AN OPEN INVITATION

You are invited. Annually, in the garden Publishing will extend a personal invitation to the world to participate in *The Journey Home* Global Collaborative Book Project.

Each volume will feature a specific theme and a variety of guest authors. Always the central theme will be a variation of the ever-expanding knowledge that each one of us is individually a unique expression of the Divine.

It is in this recognition of your true nature that one can begin to live a more balanced life in mind, body and spirit. In a renewed state of harmony within, we transform the world without.

What is required? Truly, only a shift in perception. This perceptive shift into Conscious Awareness seems to be approaching critical mass whether or not you believe any of the hype surrounding 2012.

What has been your experience? *The Journey Home*, at its core, is a collection of love letters as we travel down the path of discovery. And what an amazing journey! Won't you join us?

Follow / Participate in *The Journey Home* Annual
Global Collaborative Open Book Project by visiting
www.GroundingHeavenAsEarth.com.

The JOURNEY Home

VOLUME 1

2012

in the garden Publishing

a media company of

WHAT WOULD LOVE DO INT'L LTD

ISBN: 978-0-9855314-6-1

Library of Congress data available upon request.

Cover and Interior Design by Christine Horner

Published by:

IN THE GARDEN PUBLISHING
P.O. Box 752252
Dayton, OH 45475

www.inthegardenpublishing.com
www.whatwouldlovedointl.com

CONTENTS

INTRODUCTION

"The journey happens in the mind.
The discovery happens in the heart."

~ Mooji

This is the story of the road to nowhere; a journey of the heart, from the shadowy perception of separation to the illumination of our inherent wholeness. Some call this journey the creation of a New Earth, others the story of the return to Source.

In every case, the road Home is Life Itself, where we embrace *both* our perfect expressions of Divine Emptiness and Divine Fullness, known as the Divine Paradox.

Like many facets of the same diamond, we are the collective One, each with a sacred story to share of our journey on this road called Life. Life is not who you are, but rather an experience pointing you back toward who you are.

This year we asked our global contributors to share their thoughts on the following:

There appears to be a conscious revolution taking place. As we collectively shift into expanded awareness, what has been your experience? What have you discovered? What wisdom do you wish to share with the world? Make us laugh, cry and inspire us. How has love taken over your life? What gifts have difficult circumstances led you to discover?

We invited professional and non-professional writers alike to participate in this pilot project. And you shared. Each experience is so unique; you will be amazed at what you, the reader, will find on these pages.

You may even be inspired to begin your own journey of discovery, whether by sharing your own story, starting a journal or even simply taking regular walks in nature, asking the question, "Who am I?" And when you do, you'll...

Come home to yourself and discover Heaven on Earth.

Christine Horner, Publisher,
in the garden Publishing

Dvorah Adler (Dvorahji)

chapter 1

Dvorah Adler (Dvorahji)

I came to the United States on the General Moore, a ship that landed in New York Harbor fifty-seven years ago. My father held me on his shoulders so I could see the Statue of Liberty holding her torch of hope and welcome. We were refugees from Nazi Germany, spared from the ovens and on our way to a distant uncle in Los Angeles, who was willing to take us in and offer us citizenship. I still remember the cheers when we finally hit shore. America! We were safe.

My mother ended up working as a line-man in a Cheetos factory, and my father, a tailor, made clothes for Lucille Ball. On Saturdays my Mom and I would go downtown to get colored blouses to match the skirts my Dad made, so I'd look well-dressed for school.

I remember being eight years old, sitting alone on the grass at Queen Anne Park in South Los Angeles (we lived in a ghetto), eating my lunch, when I noticed a dozen young black boys moving toward me.

First they walked, then ran and then shouted. I froze. They encircled me; I couldn't move. I tried to get up and one of them pushed me down again. Suddenly, a huge older black man dashed up, yelling at the young boys, "Leave her alone! You punks, get outta here!" They scattered. I ran home. Saved again, but for what?

One morning, my father woke me up, "Get up Dvorah. Your Mother is in the hospital."

We rushed to the hospital. My mother had died—a heart attack at forty. One day she's making me breakfast before school, the next she's gone. I looked for her in the streets of Los Angeles for years, only to discover she was really gone. But where did she go?

That's a question that stayed with me. How can someone be here one second, and gone the next? It was all like a dream. And then the eternal questions began. What's it all about? Why am I here? How is it possible that a person, my mother could just disappear?

Years went by; I rock 'n' rolled on the Dick Clark show, graduated high school still a virgin, and at nineteen, married the first good-looking guy resembling Elvis. It was the 60s.

I remember riding my bike through Griffith Park listening to a hot local band called The Doors. I fell in love with Van Morrison. Then the L.A. riots came! I was huddled in my apartment, pregnant at twenty with my first child. What was happening in my America?

From that day on, I got involved. I marched for Civil Rights, singing "We Shall Overcome" at rallies until my throat was raw. I taught parents and preschoolers in East L.A. and Watts, while gunshots fired outside. I felt part of Martin Luther King's vision, "I have a Dream," and I was dedicated to making this a better world. My parents and I were not saved so we could eat apple pie and watch television. It had to be for a greater purpose.

One day, at a picnic with my husband and three-year-old son,

13

Chapter 1

I had a strong urge to leave immediately. "Come on, let's pack up and go! It's time to go home!"

I was so insistent that we got up, and we all walked toward the car when we heard a loud noise. We looked up and saw a car careen off the road and land up-side-down exactly where we'd been sitting. Crazy! Unbelievable. And saved again. Why?

I went to San Francisco, left my son and husband for a couple of months and marched against the war. I hung out with the underground freedom fighters, hoping to change the world—it was in a mess, AGAIN! I had never done drugs, but one day a guy handed me a joint. "Go ahead, try it. It won't hurt you." Why not, I thought. I took a couple of drags and fell asleep.

I woke up the next morning and everything looked different. I walked to Haight-Ashbury Park, looked up at the trees and sky and they were vibrating, sparkling, as was everything and everyone, including me. Things were not as they appeared to be. We were not solid. Everything blended. The Trees, the rocks, the people, my hand, we were all vibrating in unison. We were all ONE.

I went back to the apartment I was staying in and noticed a book on table. It was by Allan Watts, called *This Is It!* I took the next plane home to Los Angeles and learned to meditate. Dope was not my path, meditation was.

I became a teacher of Transcendental Meditation. I wanted to know what was real and fair in a world that seemed so unreal and so unfair. For me the ticket was looking inside this body and mind. Where else could I go for answers?

I meditated for thirty years, teaching meditation all over the world. I studied with some of the greatest Masters and Madmen and still knew nothing. I talked the Advaita talk and cried the Bhakti prayer and had the usual spiritual answers about past lives, energy, consciousness, etc. I had the rhetoric down. But I "knew" nothing. This may have been It, according to Alan Watts, but I wasn't IT!

And then, one day, a rainbow shining through a window landed on top of my hand. I looked at all the colors, mesmerized in amazement. How could something so unreal look so real?

It looked as if true colors were painted on my hand, and yet it was only a reflection. I felt a switch go off in my brain. This world is not as it appears to be. The ONENESS I'd experienced in Haight-Ashbury came flooding back. This division, this unhappiness in myself, and others, was like a mass hypnosis, an illusion, like the rainbow shining on my hand.

All I can say, is there is deep peace in the middle of this world that appears to be so chaotic, uncaring and random. There is deep knowledge that you can ONLY BE, and sounds so ridiculous and trite when you talk about it. Anyone can wake up to one's true, peaceful, enlightened nature in the midst of heartbreak and confusion. That possibility, that invitation exists for everyone.

Now if a broken little girl, who came from the heart of Hell in Nazi Germany can awaken to the heart of peace in America—I say anything is Possible.

chapter 2

Patricia Allen

PURE SURVIVOR

Struggling in defeat,

Drowning in mental tides,

The survivor thinks again,

With new thoughts, he re-decides.

We will all survive this seeming God-forsaken crucifix of an existence? We will all resurrect, having shed the cloth of these bodies, and dismissed the carnal prison of the mind?

It was only for a while we were to leave the Garden from a seeming disobedience, in order to forget our Pure Selves and then, after remembering, to get back there where we belong.

Chapter 2

God did not intend for us not to survive the tangled web of good and evil. He planned it so not only would we survive, but be even tons stronger for the experience of it all. It is like being put on a deserted island with nothing but a leaf on our private parts to figure out how to survive. And then with the fall, we hit our heads and acquired amnesia.

So, all we need do is remember. It has been a long tiresome haul trying to do it all in our failing human strength. Determined, we have fought to survive, many falling by the wayside for despair in hopeless denials; many more conquering, yet, in reality, become more deeply embedded in a quicksand from applauding its own self, alone for the triumph; and a few stand survived, in the remembering of who they really are.

These few are the appointed survivors that will lead the forgetful others by making little soft nudges to their consciousness, reminding them that they are survivors as well.

I was on the island of Maui once for a temporary stay in order for my husband to finish some legal affairs. We started out camping with the intention to rent a place, sooner rather than later.

The island was in the big middle of a big boom, with not only tourists but new residents as well. Every rental was either not available, or had long lists of applications. We had to face the fact that camping was our only option.

The first two months of camping drove me into a frenzy of yelling to God that I could not survive another day of living like that. My fingers were hurting from digging in the car for certain clothing, the showers were ice cold, my ankles were swollen from sleeping in the car, as our tent was mangled from the winter wind and rain. Basically I was not in the mood to endure such conditions.

Well, nothing changed from my yelling to God and as I conceded to the fact it may not change for a while, I made a decision to not only survive, but to survive with dignity, creativeness, and joy. That is all it took, a decision! I immediately went to the store and bought clear plastic organizers to fit perfect in the back of the car, signed up at the Salvation Army for hot showers every other day, bargained with a sales manager at a sports store for the floor model tent—the easiest tent ever to put up and take down—and started enjoying the different beaches around the island, exploring all of Maui's wondrous landscapes. It was after eight months we were able to leave and go back to the comforts of indoor living.

When I reflect back on that experience, I feel as though God put me through a form of boot camp, to survive, to conquer the negative, fearful despairs, and be ready to lead others to a creative, joyful, and exploring way in which to survive during any inconvenient circumstances and situations. A metaphoric experience that remains vivid in my consciousness, knowing there may come a day when we will all be tempted to yell at God and will need to make a new decision to survive with dignity, creativity, and joy.

The Israelites did not survive the desert because they stood fast with yelling at God, without making any new decisions. Our Divine Pure nature of Survivor is pleading the consciousness to recall itself, to rise out of the ashes of hopelessness and revel in the beauty of creativity and joy, into the experience of exploring into a new decision, to survive.

We do not live on bread alone and it takes much more than mere food and water to survive.

You are Pure Survivor! Let Divine Pure Survivor, creatively, and decisively survive!

chapter 3

Marilee Bresciani, Ph.D

Self-Love...what is self-love? Well, what is love? I didn't really know what self-love was...maybe I still don't. I am pretty sure I know what the experience of love feels like, however, and when I focus on that—when I focus on how the experience of love feels—I can better translate it to the experience of love for myself. But how can I be sure what self-love is? To quote my dear friend Marva—literacy professor, artist, dancer, doting mother, devoted friend, one who knows how to invite cancer out of the body, and Love role model—sometimes it is helpful in discovering what something *is* by exploring what it *is not*.

Do you remember the "Love is..." comic strip? The strip featured a naked, gender-neutral character. Each one-frame strip shared in a very simple way what love is in the many forms that love can show up. I was drawn to the comic strip. It made me feel good, even though I didn't always understand the message. I smiled when

I read it...that was up until the day I didn't smile while reading it. That day coincided with the realization that my marriage was failing. All of a sudden, I found myself not believing that love existed and so I no longer smiled at the comic strip. What I didn't realize in that moment was, what had really happened is that my former husband and I hadn't fallen out of love with each other; I had fallen out of love with myself.

Thus, began my journey of exploring what love *is not*. And this is what I discovered and am still discovering in my journey.

Love is not about sacrifice; it is about choice. I was brought up to be my own person while also making sure that I was aware and sensitive to the needs of those around me. I am grateful for being brought up this way. The challenge I experienced, however, is that I chose to be more sensitive to the needs of those around me than to trust my own needs. I thought that this was what love was. I thought that if I were truly loving, I would sacrifice my own needs and desires for those around me. I didn't know that all that would do would be to lead me down a path of inauthenticity and growing resentment of whom I was and who I was becoming.

We are taught that if we truly love someone, we will sacrifice who we are and what we want for their needs. But if you think about that, it makes no sense at all. All that kind of thinking does is contribute to increasing demands and expectations of one another. With this kind of thinking, people have conversations that begin with, "If you really loved me, you would... [fill in the blank with all the things you have either said aloud or thought silently to yourself when disappointed by another's behavior. Or fill this in with all the things others have said to you in your life]. Are you feeling kind of stressed right now? I am.

Now turn this around for a moment and begin by asking yourself, "If I really loved myself, I would... [Fill in with one of the answers that follows or create your own] 1) ask for the help I need, 2) tell the other person I love in a compassionate way that what he/she is asking me to do is incredibly uncomfortable, 3) tell the person I love in a compassionate way that I need to tend to this first before I can tend to their need so that I can be fully present for them, 4) just say no.

When I began practicing this turnaround, I found myself incredibly empowered to make my own choices about taking care of myself first. In taking care of myself first, I decreased the stress I created in my life. I also decreased the expectations that I had on others, which allowed more freedom for them to show up in love as their authentic selves. This practice also provided clarity for me to make conscious "sacrifices" for another, which decreased my resentment of decisions I made. Putting myself first gave me room to more freely and fully express my love for others, rather than be in a constant mind-battle and heart-battle about whether I was meeting their expectations for me without regard for how their expectations were affecting my own well-being, my own inner peace, my own wellspring of love. Furthermore, beginning to focus on what I needed to do for me first, allowing myself to discover how well I was I was meeting my own expectations for myself or whether I was even clear on what those were.

The love relationship begins with oneself as we genuinely inquire into who we are and what we need. Owning those answers, we can move forward in authentic relationship with another, asking for what we need from them and vice versa, while letting each other know what we are capable of and/or willing to provide to each other. It doesn't mean that another won't have an expectation for me, but I can more quickly realize that the expectation is theirs to own. I can engage in a conversation with them about their expectation of me, and let them know how I am willing or not willing to meet their expectation of me. They can choose to re-engage in the "if you love me, you will..." conversation. All the while I can hear that and turn it around and say, "If I love me, I will respond to this expectation in this way so that I can maintain the peaceful relationship I have with myself and my journey toward the greater good."

Love is not about getting sexually aroused; it is about knowing what to do when sexually aroused that will honor the greater good. I very much enjoy the feelings I get when I am sexually aroused and I enjoy seeing a man get aroused in my presence if I am also aroused by him. I used to mistake sexual arousal for love. I recognize you may be laughing at me right now, but I honestly have never been able to simply have a one-night stand with someone. For me, having sex with someone means getting emotionally involved with them; having sex with someone for me means I am going to be around to be a good friend to you until the time when I feel your presence in my life is not honoring my journey, and when our relationship is not honoring the greater good. If I experience sex with someone and then he chooses to leave my life abruptly, the relationship feels incomplete, the lessons unlearned, the union feels that it has ended unresolved, and my heart is deeply saddened (a.k.a. one-night stands).

I enjoy the feeling of being aroused. My physical arousal signifies to me that I am drawn to this person for more than their outward appearance. There is something within them that is calling to something within me. And my response to that unspoken calling is arousal. I used to think that having sex with someone meant that you had to have a commitment of love with that person—even if it were the "love at first sight" kind of thing. But later in life, during the time I no longer smiled at the "Love is" comic strip, I came to realize that someone *can* have sex with another person without an emotional commitment. Someone *can* have sex with another for the simple pleasure of experiencing sex. I realized that it would best benefit me and my relationship with myself to not judge that—to not judge that someone can engage in sex with another and without experiencing any emotional connection whatsoever. However, to honor the relationship with myself, I needed to acknowledge that I was not one of those folks—again no judgment on me or anyone not like me. As much as I enjoy great sex, it is only great for me if there is an emotional connection with the one in whom I am completely engaged.

When I feel sexual arousal, I appreciate that I sense something in another that invites a union with each other, yet unions come in many forms. Just because I am sexually aroused by another does not mean that I will engage in intercourse, experience an emotional connection, or experience Love with that person.

It may mean to quote my dear friend, David—man of action, man of great wisdom, man of deep spiritual connectivity, my personal protector, and another beautiful Love role model—that we are drawn to each other to teach and learn from each other in that moment or perhaps in a later moment.

The sexual draw to one another may mean that we are to share lessons of the intellect, the spirit, the soul, or the mind. It may also just be about experiencing a desire for sexual pleasure with each other. Or perhaps it signals to me that I am desiring a union with myself—a loving of myself (and I am not talking dildo here; I mean the deep union of mind, body, and soul that comes in meditation or the practice of silence). Or it may mean something else. The question is do you know what the sexual arousal is signaling to you to explore?

The strong feelings and yearnings for sexual union may be present in a love relationship or they may be present outside of a loving relationship. Simply notice your sexual arousal—without judgment—and invite yourself to inquire within yourself about how best to manifest those desires in the way that honors your relationship with yourself first and foremost. Then invite yourself to inquire as to whether your decision honors the greater good. And then simply enjoy the results and/or consequences of your decision.

Love is not something to be gotten; it is to be experienced in the journey of relationship with oneself. I often hear people say how much they need love in their life. I have often said this and I could be the poster child for the song entitled, "Looking For Love In All The Wrong Places." And what I have learned through this immense heartache is that love is to be experienced in our moment-to-moment choices. Love is to be experienced in the journey of relationship with ourselves.

Experiencing love is experiencing self-love pure and simple. In every moment of every day, if we could just consciously choose to answer the question what is the most loving thing I can do for myself in this moment that also serves the greater good, and then choose that—oh my heaven, we would experience lasting peace and joy in that moment. How cool would that be? And while others around us may look at us as if we are insane, we would know in our heart and soul that we have just loved our self deeply and as a result, we wouldn't feel the their judgment in that moment. We only feel the judgment of others when we move out of that place of self-referral (e.g., what is the most loving thing I can do for myself in this moment that serves the greater good?), to discover that the person or people around us have expectations for us about how we can serve them (e.g. If you loved me, you would…).

So, while the solution is easy, the practice is challenging because, at least for me, I have forty-seven years of unconscious choice-making to undo. I need to practice inquiring into how I feel and what I sense in the moment. I need to stop reacting to instinctively pleasing another and stop to ask what is the most loving thing I can do for myself in this moment that serves the greater good. In inquiring into how to be most loving to me while considering the greater good, I am considering the other loved ones in my life as well, even though they may not feel like it because their demands are not overriding my own internal wisdom for myself.

Please understand that none of this means that you "go it alone". I love the story that Byron Katie tells about needing a hug. One day, she and her husband were standing on a crowded street corner and she got this overwhelming need to be hugged. So, she asked her husband if he would hug her. Because he was rather distracted at the moment, he declined her request. She was not angry with him or resentful of her need, she simply turned to the stranger next to her and asked him to give her a hug and he graciously complied. Both Byron Katie and the stranger got their needs met and it served the greater good for both of them as well as her husband because he was present to her receiving the hug from the stranger—the hug that he just wasn't in the space to give. I love this story. To me it signifies owning what you need from others without placing blame or expectations on them to give it to you. And it also signifies not denying what you do need others to provide. I have hugged myself when I needed a hug—it doesn't quite do the trick.

It is true that no one knows you better than you, so join me in not expecting others to provide for you what you need. Rather, check in with yourself and ask another person for what you need of them. Invite them into their own self-love journey and challenge each other together to love oneself as you experience loving the other. Love is experiencing love by journeying into your own self-love relationship. Enjoy the journey; enjoy the adventure. Namaste!

* * *

Dr. Marilee Bresciani can be reached at mbrescia@mail.sdsu.edu or at rushingtoyoga@gmail.com

chapter 4

Michiel Broeren

The Journey I Am: Riding the Waves of Change

Throughout my life dealing with change has been a returning issue. I strive to change things I don't like about my life or about my character. Or I fight against changes that come my way that I don't want to be taking place. I constantly seem to be in a space where I either need to improve myself in some way or defend myself against things I don't want to happen. Whenever I have (or think I have) failed to influence the course of events, there's the need to come to terms with all that actually has occurred in spite of what I strived or wished for.

Living between hope and fear

Hope and fear are the main drivers of this attitude. In all this striving for change, I've been hoping to create a better life for myself. In following up on my hope, I make use of a belief system that tells me that if I can create the desired change, at some point in my life I will reach a state of being where everything will be largely in order. Although I always accepted that there still will be ups and downs in life, I unconsciously also believe that I can reach a better position in life than the one I'm holding now. I've been looking for enlightenment or at least a degree of spiritual mastery that will take me to a position of abundant joy, wealth, health and love. I perceive that space as "the place where I really belong" or even "home". I also notice that in spite of my growing wisdom and ability to surrender to things throughout the years, I still dislike certain turns my life has been taking. Some things I just don't want to happen and I (tried to) resist the change that occurred. Fear is a main driver here like the fear to be a failure, to be weak, to be considered overwhelming or to be overwhelmed myself. These fears have to ensure my survival and prevent me from becoming poor, ill, socially isolated or dead.

Home is here and now

At times I find that I'm not controlled by these forces of hope and fear. I find myself in the position of an observer; I look at my life from a slight distance and lose attachment with what goes on for a moment. I lose my judgments on things and have the ability to look at life in acceptance of what it is.

Being in that space, a moment came where I could embrace that being home is here, right now and right in this space. Home is the recognition that I'm already enlightened. I'm already a whole being and there's nothing to be done to achieve anything, improve anything or grow spiritually. The whole experience that I call my human life is home: this is it!

Of course, I've read those statements before, but in the seat of the observer I could actually feel it: this is it and it's perfect in its tremendous beauty of simplicity, kindness and completeness.

Every moment of joy, pain, feeling hot or cold, nervous, jealous, sexy or fit is completely me. My roles as a father, a writer, a husband, a life coach, a trainer, a friend, an angry driver or a malcontent customer. All the moods that arise in me, followed by actions like being polite, being friendly, being loving, being angry, aggressive, open, closed, kind, heartless: it's all the divine me.

This discovery struck me with a strong degree of fear and dislike at first. Apathy grabbed hold of me. If this is it, everything as it is now is totally perfect, than what's the point of being here? What's the point if there's nothing left to hope for, nothing to be done, nothing to be achieved? The flaws in my character are perfect; that's not easy to accept. And am I supposed to simply accept illness, depression or anxiety? And even if I feel my "true love" or happiness, it's just an experience that is only a small part of reality. If that is supposed to make me feel like I've discovered paradise, I don't think I like paradise all that much.

As time went by I realized that if everything is just perfect as it is, being here in a human manifestation is also perfect in all its aspects. In this human experience I perceive all kinds of joys, fears, drives, belief systems, wants and needs. So that must be perfect too. Even if I try, one thing can't be prevented. Things happen; there is a constant stream of events. I see myself doing things, I see others doing things. I breathe, talk, make decisions to buy something, take a job, rent a house or whatnot.

My moods change whether I like it or not. I grow older and my physical appearance changes. My insights also change. My perception of things is constantly shifting and presenting me with new ways to look at life experiences. Everything is simply constantly on the move, both inside and outside of me. I also act constantly in this human experience. I simply cannot not move.

The illusion of choice

I've become aware that I believe that I can influence what happens in my life by making choices. To some extent that's true, of course. Every action I take has effect. I can decide to do something or not and both decisions will have a different turn of events as an effect. The hard thing to accept however is that in reality I have no idea what the outcome of my choices will be. All I know is that they have effect. I try to predict what that effect will be but in all honesty I can't predict what will happen at all.

This leads to the awareness at the same time that my choices are fairly insignificant. Nothing I do is a guarantee for any outcome. I'm at the mercy of forces bigger than me. I don't possess the ability to oversee what my choices and non-chosen actions will lead to; I notice my mind constantly creates a difference between what is and what should be.

The gap that is experienced through that system is what I experience as the distance still to be covered. There is no distance to be covered. Everything is there simultaneously and without any timeframe. There isn't a positive and a negative side to things. Everything is simply always present at the same time. All that I am, my whole being, is fully here in this now moment that is best described as the present.

There's no preferred space or position to be in because that simply isn't possible: I'm (in) all experiences at the same time. In this human experience I do not possess the helicopter view to see this. In my perception I seem to hold a relative position in the experience. This perception easily leads to a belief that I have a choice in my position in life.

Stronger still, it can easily lead to the illusion that it's my choices that are the cause for what goes on in my life. But in reality I don't have the rational power to make "the right choice" in terms of choosing in such a way that I will be sure of where my choice will take me. If I accept that as true, it's logical that I also can't make "the wrong choice".

There is a force in me however that "knows" without ratio what to go for and what to leave out. I have the ability to distinguish between what makes my energy grow and flow and what actions make it smaller or even stall. That is what really triggers me to make choices. The energy that I am makes itself known at all times. I can move "with it" or "against it," which creates different noticeable effects. The energy I am presents itself in different chains of events all the time. I often perceive these different manifestations as change.

Change and the unchangeable core

Change is the most wonderful aspect of the human experience. The only certainty that human life truly presents is that everything changes all the time. The moment of my conception was immediately a moment of change. A sperm made connection with an ovule and from that moment on the human 'me' was starting to become materialized through a process of change. Every moment of my existence, smaller and bigger changes have occurred on a physical, emotional and/or intellectual level. This process will continue. In the materialized manifestation that I perceive as my human life, one thing is constantly clear: everything is always on the move.

Yet one aspect of "me" is unchangeable. If I try to describe this aspect of my being words come like "I'm just a source of energy." It's a non-material part of my existence, and yet I clearly notice its presence. It's the presence of the observer in me, a force that can look at (my) life from a so called meta position. This source is free of judgment, in acceptance of all that is, untouchable, unable to be touched and also unable to be corrupted or changed in any way. It's a very tranquil space where I lose the urge to provoke or prevent any of life's movements.

My mind wants to navigate me

I'm equipped with a mind that supports me in this human experience. The mind is the computer that gathers all information provided by the complex system of my human body and can use this information (received in the form of neurotic incentives) to make my body move, breathe, sleep, walk, talk and whatnot.

This mind has the curious habit of trying to understand the experiences I'm in as well. It tries to perform the task of navigating me through this experience. In order to do that, it develops a chart or layout to be able to determine my position. It creates this chart by developing an ever-growing set of definitions and norms that help me to know where I am, who I am and what I'm doing.

This in turn helps to explain why I feel in a certain way, why things happen to me and why I should or shouldn't do things. This creates a sense of clarity or even control over my life. The mind however does not realize one thing: it's an instrument of hindsight and interpretation. In reality I've no idea who I am, where I am or even what I am. There's no materialized "me". I'm just "energy" if you even can call it that: I simply am. There's no reason to my being, no why, I just am. I know nothing on forehand.

The mind believes it registers things as they are happening but that isn't so. Things simply happen and only when (and thus after) they do, does it become possible to reflect on them with my intellect. The mind reconstructs what happens into a logical story all on its own accord. This reconstruction doesn't have anything to do with "the reality": it's simply an attempt to create a "grip" on life. From this "grip" or understanding, the mind starts to predict what will happen in the future if I act in a certain way. In reality I don't have any grip and there's no way to predict the future.

There's nothing I can do to truly influence the everlasting wave of changing energy that I am and that I live in. I'm equipped with the ability to simply float on that wave of energy! But it's a (life-long) journey of letting go, of un-creating that I buy into my belief systems of navigation that enables me to really fully ride that wave. That's where I truly come home.

I know nothing

Many unexpected turns in life, ups and downs, teach me to have deep reverence for the depth of my not-knowing. I've learned that I know nothing, nothing can be a prediction for how the future will present itself: I truly have no control whatsoever.

Even the statement that I do have control over my attitude towards what goes on in my life is only partially true. Yes, most of the time I have the illusion that I can influence my mood by staying "positive" or "strong". But at times panic, apathy or rage simply take over and leave me with nothing but the option to ride those waves of energy as well. I'm also equipped with the intuitive power to make choices, and they can feel like they're deeply motivated by my "higher self" or spirit. But I don't really know this for sure. I truly know nothing, and I learn to deeply bow to all that is without any judgment or inclination to create change.

I see myself

Yet there's one "knowing" that I do have: I know how I perceive things from my unique perspective. I see me and I have the ability to share how I experience things. In this human life there appears to be a separation between me and "others". Although I may have experiences that "we're all one", I also experience moments of separation and loneliness. My perspective from this separated space is totally unique and yet, when I give words or other forms of expression to my perspective, those "others" have the remarkable ability to comprehend me. Although I know nothing about life in general, I do have knowledge about my own perspective. By expressing that knowledge that isn't rational a lot of the times, I can create bridges that resolve my separation.

Being open

By being open about all that is alive inside of me, I become more transparent. Whenever I openly express how I perceive things, experiences become more alive, they seem to change quicker and appear with more diversion. If I'm in a situation I don't enjoy and I'm open about it, movement in this situation occurs much more quickly. And if I express my joy with a situation, the experience of joy gets a chance to deepen or multiply itself. The problem for my defense systems (my mind) being of course that there's no telling what responses I'm actually provoking by being open!

Being open to chances and change is not a doing. Change and creating new chances are the result of being open about my inner world, about what I perceive in the present moment.

Surrendering to that simple truth means expressing and acting on what I perceive without having to obtain any set outcome. This conscious attitude of not knowing anything for sure, not pretending to understand anything about life but simply trusting my inner wisdom creates new opportunities and experiences beyond my wildest dreams!

Sweet surrender

Just being, that's all that life is about. Being in sweet surrender with what is. There's nothing else to do. In essence becoming alive is about un-creating all the systems that tell me that I need to do something. I know nothing, not about others and not about myself. I don't need any navigation system. The mind can rest at ease. There's no road and there are no hazards to be avoided so I can simply be. In my core I'm untouchable. I cannot perish, be damaged or destroyed. In my true state of being I'm equipped to be with whatever comes my way in this human experience. By being open I create constant movement. At the same time I don't have to direct myself towards any set outcome. Whenever I can surrender to that loving truth, I am truly free.

* * *

Michiel Broeren is a Life Coach and the author of *Living in Trust*. You can find Michiel at www.alivecoaching.nl or www.alive.net.nz

chapter 5

Trey Carland

Fear of Life

As you may already know, my wife, Shelby, is pregnant again. Needless to say, there is a new air of excitement going around as this new addition grows in her mother's warm and loving belly. Yes, that's right, it's a girl.

So far, the baby seems to be doing well with no noticeable health issues. She's very active in there, too. Every time Shelby feels kicks and flips I can't help but think about how crazy that must be. There's a little human being in there flailing about, learning how to operate their tiny little limbs. It's just miraculous. I'm getting to feel and see the movements, too.

It's been a little over a year since we lost our first little girl, Stella Grace, and we've found ourselves on almost the exact same schedule. Sprout (our nickname for new baby-to-be) is estimated to arrive on April 20, 2012, while Stella was estimated to arrive on April 17, 2011. I don't think Sprout is going to wait until her due date to come, so she could well be born on her sister's due date. Pregnancies after a loss tend to be experienced a bit differently anyway, but having the same schedule makes it seem even more special. After a loss, the innocence of what can go wrong is gone, and is replaced with the burden of knowing the myriad of things that do go wrong.

The loss of innocence can be painful, and may leave behind a permanent scar. It also leaves behind a changed perspective on life. In complete innocence there is no fear, and in a state of no fear there is peace. After innocence is damaged, fear is born. Fear wants to protect us from harm so that we may enjoy peace once again, but fear and peace cannot coexist. A return to innocence will bring about peace, but past experience has told us that it is dangerous to allow ourselves to be that vulnerable again. We remember being hurt when we were innocent, and the mind points to those painful experiences to justify the need for fear. The mistake here is the false belief that fear could have protected us from the pain incurred by a loss of innocence.

Fear can't really protect us from anything, except maybe peace. Though that makes perfect sense, believing it doesn't make fear go away. Experience tells us that there is no end to the number of things that could potentially go "wrong" in any given life, before or after birth, which is why many of us live in fear of life, or, put another way, we fear living a life without fear. We "know" too much to be fully at ease all the time. So let's look at what we "know" at the root of this fear.

Life is Scary

For example, you never know what's going to happen from one minute to the next. Something bad always happens when I let my guard down. If I don't worry I won't be ready when the worst-case scenario happens. If I allow myself to fully relax I'm putting too much trust in a life that can't be trusted. Life has let me down so many times I can't even count. I'm scared of not knowing what's going to happen next. I'm angry that I can't ensure things turn out the way I want. I don't know what to do. I don't want to have to worry, or keep my guard up, but trusting life might jinx the outcome.

Is That True?

Pain is unavoidable in this life, but what if it's completely necessary? What if our suffering is part of a master plan? What if this master plan has our best interest at heart? Is it possible to put trust in life's plan? How does it feel to let down your guard and trust life? Sit with that last question and really experience letting your guard down about a particularly stressful situation. What does it feel like to surrender? Do you experience fear? Loss? Relief? Joy? Resistance? Do you want to cry? Laugh? Both? Just sit with that experience of allowing yourself to be completely vulnerable, without judging yourself or the situation. [I highly recommend Gina Lake's book, "Trusting Life."]

Looking Inside

An interesting thing about fear is that it typically has a bodily sensation that goes with it. When you are experiencing some sort of stress or fear, check in with your body to see if there is any tension. Once you locate it, direct your attention to that area of the body.

Feel that tension and allow it to be there, fully. Give yourself permission to be tense. There is absolutely nothing wrong with any physical or emotional response that you have. Welcome it all and see how that feels.

I was reminded of this mind-body connection at a recent satsang with Benjamin Smythe (http://www.benjamintsmythe.com), while we were talking about the fear of life. Benjamin is known for traveling around with a large sign that says, "You're Perfect!" He finds a public place to sit or stand and just holds the sign up to people walking by. He gets a wide range of responses, ranging from gratitude to indifference to anger. The thing is, he no longer cares what kind of response he gets. As he will tell you, his fear is gone (enlightenment has a tendency to do that to a person ;-).

During the satsang I told him that I had some fear of life in me, and asked if I should go stand somewhere holding a sign like him. We all had a good chuckle, but then he asked if I had any fear at that moment. I admitted that I did have a little (sort of like a mild stage fright you might get if you were admitting a perceived weakness in front of a large group of people). He told me to check in with my body to see if I could feel any tension. I located some tightness in my thighs and my upper arms, and relayed that information. He congratulated me and invited me to completely allow that tension to be there. As soon as I did I started laughing. I was instantly able to see through the fear. It was just an illusion. Benjamin explained that dealing with fear may be more easily dealt with on the physical level because the mind is what created it in the first place, and it's hard to get the creator of fear to alleviate it.

So What?

How does all of this serve me in my current life situation, dealing with a potentially stressful pregnancy? One key is to take things one day at a time (remain present). During a recent event that caused us some concern about the baby, my mind became a fear monger of "What if," scenarios. I could not shake the thoughts, but I could feel the tension being created in my body. The tension was not localized, and could be felt all over. This time noticing it and allowing it did not give me the same relief. What I did instead is recognized the thoughts as just thoughts, not reality. This enabled me to relax for brief periods, but I was unable to be fully at ease until we had our visit with the Nurse and learned everything was fine.

There will always be life situations like this that have the ability to engender fear. Accepting fear when it occurs (instead of resisting it) is very important. However, realizing that the root of the fear is believing our thoughts is even more important. Once that's realized, the thoughts can be looked at impartially as part of the human condition, not as if they were true.

After writing this, I felt moved to write a couple of poems.

The End of Fear

In the end, there was the beginning

A circle brought to life, only not to end

Where am I to go?

Trapped in eternity

Scared to stop

Scared to move forward

Unable to do either

43

Unable to do both

Where am I to go?

Nowhere but here

What about fear?

There is only fear if you allow there to be

Turn your attention toward it

See if that fear is real

Electrical impulses given a four letter word is all that's really there

Being trapped, unable to move or stop, are just concepts

The domino effect of belief ends in fear

Fear ends in the recognition of its origin

The Last Step

This moment has already happened

And it's already gone

Can we change what's already happened?

What's now has already passed

Now becomes the past in the blink of an eye

It seems to leave evidence that it used to exist

Pictures and memories

Traces of things that seem to have moved

But how do we know the past actually was?

Look around

Are you still where you were?

It seems like it

Have you ever really moved?

It seems like it

Haven't you always been where you were?

I don't know

Seconds leave a blurry trail of seeming reality

But are seconds really real though?

What does it really mean when we say "ago"?

That blurry trail of time goes on for years and years

Until we start to forget and the trail begins to disappear

Let the earth beneath your feet crumble as your feet take a step

Let every step be the last

Let every step be the first

* * *

Trey Carland can be found at www.treycarland.com

chapter 6

Jed Diamond, Ph.D

My Father, My Son: On Love and Loss

It didn't look like I was going to make it into the world and it looked like my father was on his way out. My birth was somewhat of a miracle when I was born on December 21st. My parents had been trying to conceive, without success for nine years. Their doctor recommended a procedure of injecting my father's sperm into my mother's womb. It worked and my mother was ecstatic to be having a baby. She told stories of walking carefully down the streets of Greenwich Village in New York trying to insure that she didn't lose this new life growing inside her. But my father was becoming increasingly depressed because he now had a family to support and the job market looked grim for a writer and actor in New York City.

He described his hopes and growing despair in a journal I found in the attic of our house on Hesby Street in Los Angeles many years later:

Chapter 6

<u>April 15th</u>

"A traveling troupe is putting on a show not far from us. I know them from earlier times when I first came to New York. They are gay and exciting and have an enchanting flavor of holiday. I look at Kath and marvel at her sweetness and beauty. You often forget how lovely feminine youth is. The cream-like texture of skin, a verve and a buoyancy. Henry is a perfect type of company manager. He has great big floppy ears, that inevitable cigar, and a certain softness. Charm is not the exclusive province of youth. Henry has it as well as Kath.

"Kath has that wonderful spirit of newness about her, that same wide-eyed wonder that a child has when he is seeing the circus for the first time. She sits at the feet of the elders who have been around the block and have makeup rubbed into their soles (sic). She reminds me of my little boy [I was five at the time]. He has a wonderful impishness, a beautiful delightful growth about him. He has a suppleness of mind and body, a rapt attention as he looks for animals and calls to them.

"I feel full of confidence in my writing ability. I know for certain that someone will buy one of my radio shows. I know for certain that I will get a good part in a play. Last night I dreamt about candy. There was more candy than I could eat. Does it mean I'll be rewarded for all my efforts? Has it anything to do with sex?"

Journal number four was written three years later. The economic depression of the time and the depression going on within his mind had come together. His entries are more terse, staccato, and disheartening. I still get tears when I feel how much was lost in such a short time.

<u>June 4th</u>

"Your flesh crawls, your scalp wrinkles when you look around and see good writers, established writers, writers with credits a block long, unable to sell, unable to find work, Yes, it's enough to make anyone, blanch, turn pale and sicken."

August 15th

"Faster, faster, faster, I walk. I plug away looking for work, anything to support my family. I try, try, try, try, try. I always try and never stop."

November 8th

"A hundred failures, an endless number of failures, until now, my confidence, my hope, my belief in myself, has run completely out. Middle aged, I stand and gaze ahead, numb, confused, and desperately worried. All around me I see the young in spirit, the young in heart, with ten times my confidence, twice my youth, ten times my fervor, twice my education.

"I see them all, a whole army of them, battering at the same doors I'm battering, trying in the same field I'm trying. Yes, on a Sunday morning in early November, my hope and my life stream are both running desperately low, so low, so stagnant, that I hold my breath in fear, believing that the dark, blank curtain is about to descend."

Six days after his November entry, my father tried to kill himself. Though he survived physically, emotionally he was never again the same. It's probably not surprising that I grew up and became a psychotherapist who specializes in men's work. I've treated more and more men who are facing similar stresses to those my father experienced. The economic conditions and social dislocations that contributed to his feelings of shame and hopelessness continue to weigh heavily on men today. I wanted a better world for my children.

On another November day my wife was about to give birth to our first child and she had convinced me to take child-birth classes with her to get us both ready for the blessed event. When I began the classes, I wasn't sure I wanted to be part of the birth process. In truth, I was afraid I might pass out at the sight of the blood or become overly concerned with her pain and be more of a problem than a support.

When she was wheeled into the delivery room, the doctor asked me to leave. I experienced a mixture of sadness and relief. Following doctor's orders, I dutifully squeezed my wife's hand, turned, and walked down the long hallway toward the exit sign leading to the waiting room to sit with the other expectant fathers. Yet in the eternity of those few moments it took to make the journey out, something shifted in me. I felt a call from some deep part of myself—or maybe it was from the life preparing to come into the world. It was a call that could not be denied.

I turned around and walked into the delivery room and took my place at the head of the table. There was no question of asking permission, no chance I would leave if asked. I was simply there. I felt a wonderful calm come over me and a sense of unbelievable wonder as my son, Jemal, came into the world. My tears flowed freely as I joined in the magic of life and silently made a commitment to myself and my son that our relationship would be different than my father's had been with me and that I would do everything in my power to create the kind of world where fathers and children didn't lose connection with each other.

Following my father's suicide attempt, he was sent to Camarillo State Hospital. I still remember the big trees lining the road as my uncle Harry drove us to visit him each Sunday. At first he seemed glad to see us and appeared to be getting better. But as time went on he received electro-shock treatments which were supposed to help with his depression. His condition worsened. He became increasingly agitated and angry and didn't seem to know me or my mother. We stopped coming for visits. It was just too painful, but my uncle hung in there until the end.

The doctors told us that my father would probably never get better and would never leave the hospital. However, my father had different ideas. On one of the visits my uncle had taken him into town for a meal and some window shopping. My father said he needed to get stamps in the local post office. When my uncle went to look for him, he had disappeared. My father, Morris Diamond, was never heard from again.

I spent most of my adult life feeling the pain of his loss and wondering if I would end up in a mental hospital and if my life would end in tragedy. I still wonder, but the fear has faded over the years, helped greatly by my father's reappearance. My uncle ran into him without, at first, seeing him. The sign read, "Tommy the puppet-man, a show for our lives." My uncle stopped to watch, as puppets appeared and disappeared behind a hand-made stage. After the show the puppeteer came out from behind the curtain. It was my father. He had changed his name to Tommy Roberts and called himself "the puppet man."

My uncle wrote to me saying that he'd found my long-lost father and encouraged me to visit him. By then I was grown with my own family and looked forward, with some apprehension, to seeing him. When we met I learned that he had changed his name when he escaped the mental hospital, afraid they would capture him and return him to "the nuthouse." He had been making a living as a street puppeteer and had become quite well known on college campuses everywhere between Los Angeles and San Francisco.

He met my wife and family, and my own children had a chance to see him do his puppet shows. Our son, Jemal, grew up to be a writer and poet like his grandfather. Our daughter, Angela, expresses her creative spirit in the love and kindness she shows everyone, particularly her own three children. I continue to write books on men's health. In my latest book, I share my own journey and that of my father. He died not too long ago and I still miss him.

At his funeral I read one of his many poems:

Resiliency

Resiliency—One of Human Kind's finest graces—

Time and time and time without end

Life bends us, twists us, knots us, stretches us

Out and out and out

Till we're positive we're going to break

But out of pains and agonies, our heartaches

We snap back and go on

That power and strength to be stretched and stretched

And stretched, and then to snap back

Again and again and again

And go on

And live on

Jed Diamond, Ph.D

Of all Human Kind's finest graces, one of the finest is Resiliency.

* * *

Dr. Jed Diamond's web sites are:

www.MenAlive.com
www.SurvivingMaleMenopause.com
www.TheIrritableMale.com

chapter 7

John Suchman-Harrison

Here comes the Savior (me)! But where's mine? I know they are "out there"…somewhere.

If only I could find that person . . . that Socrates, that Mr. Miyagi—the person who would somehow just discover me and devote their time in teaching me about life.

If only I could find that person . . . that damsel-in-distress, that woman that I could rescue and give all of my love to. That would complete me! Those were the predominant thoughts of my youth.

As a ten-year-old I became "fractured". I played it off the best that I could; however, it did really get to me. Altering the perception and foundation of such a young boy were the words "your dad is not your dad."

Chapter 7

It was further explained that he is my dad, he loves me the same as my dad, but that he didn't "father" me. Well who did? I got to see some pictures. What happened as a result? I was told the story. Where is he? Nobody knew.

Meanwhile, in the coming months, I was moved from Virginia to Michigan—leaving behind my childhood love. "One day I'll come back for you," is what I thought. I was able to see her again, at fifteen, a couple of times while on a family visit (got my first kiss)—and again at nineteen when I drove to North Carolina with a friend for a couple of days (and had our unrealized last kiss).

Excuses galore on my part: I had a child in Michigan that I wouldn't leave. She hadn't graduated yet. Our time had passed.

In truth, there was only one honest reason . . . in no way could a relationship have ended my seeking.

Receiving her love, in addition to having mine received, was not at all what I wanted. As much as I believed differently, I wanted the search. Unknowingly at the time, a relationship was not what I was searching for at all.

I spent many nights wondering where I came from, what my dad was like, where he was, if he was rich and thinking that he was my Socrates. I, admittedly, forgot about him for extended lengths of time. However, I found and met him, at 22 years of age, and the seeking persisted . . . still. I now had Socrates to meet. The mind is always telling us there is something more. Which we interpret as us lacking something. And this lack leaves us thinking that we are not enough. When we feel that we are not enough, then nothing is enough. And we keep searching.

Ten years old was an important age for me. It is when I had my only dream of Jesus.

That dream consisted of me telling him that I love him and him saying "I love you, too." His response seemed appropriate for a child/soul/entity/being that could think itself was separate from Love. However, if I could re-script that dream, it would be an edit to Jesus' line. Simply stated he would say, "You need to love you. Only then can—and will—you love all else."

When you love all else, you are Home.

chapter 8

Michael Landis

Disconnecting the Buttons

"If you hold me in the palm of your hand, I will give you the world."

I feared this opportunity. I knew my options. I could walk away. And guarantee that my life would continue to slide into oblivion. Or I could let him in. A man, homeless, almost twice my age, who I knew would push every button I had.

The Matrix hadn't been released yet. If it had, I would have heard Trinity saying, "You've been down there, Neo. You know exactly where it ends."

I took him in.

My world turned upside down.

And I am forever grateful for that experience.

Chapter 8

What does it look like to awaken? For me, it started without me even knowing it. I had no near-death experiences; I didn't lose anyone near or dear to me. Instead, I slid into it sideways.

A friend of mine from college took a three-day class on self-awareness. He shared his experience with me and several others, and I was drawn to it, eventually taking three follow-up courses as well.

In the final course, we were warned that people taking this course frequently had profound experiences within six or twelve months of completing the course. I finished that course, and forgot the warning immediately.

About six months later, I met Steve at a book store. We had seen each other once before and thought nothing of it, but this time I was drawn to speak with him. He seemed sad, and I wanted to help.

We ended up talking for six hours. In that talk, he shared with me how he viewed the world: reincarnation, the power of our thoughts upon our reality, his search for his soul mate, how his power, when misused by others, ended up destroying them.

He had an uncanny knack for showing me what I didn't want to see. At one point, he kissed me. I was shocked. I told him I wasn't looking for a homosexual relationship. He responded, "Then why did I taste the coffee you had been drinking? I didn't drink any coffee."

I couldn't escape that, without thinking, I went into the kiss. I hadn't withdrawn.

Damn.

It was at this point that my awakening process became real. I had to face myself.

Eric Hop makes a valuable distinction between oneness and awakening. He describes "oneness" as the intense sensation of being part of everything, of the mind going completely still. This incredible awareness, of the world rushing in without processing, is an amazing experience that many people discover, especially in "kundalini rising" episodes and near-death experiences. Eventually it subsides, returning us to the day-to-day world of bills and deadlines and sharp elbows—the world of duality, separateness.

"Awakening," on the other hand, is a process. It's letting the ego take a passenger seat in our journey, detaching the buttons that cause us to react with anger, happiness, and so on. As we become more aware and awake, we find that our thoughts, our buttons, have much less sway over us. Everything becomes amazing, even events we would label "happy" or "sad." We no longer attach judgment on circumstances or people. We find ourselves loving everything and everyone.

The work can be quite difficult. We don't enjoy facing our shortcomings, our "poor" choices, our hurtful knee-jerk responses. And yet, somehow, as we continue to awaken, we come to appreciate and enjoy the process.

It took me a long time to get to that point.

Steve moved in with me a month after we met. The first two years with him were the most difficult years of my life. He was empathic, so he could tell when I was lying to him. I would say, "I feel fine about this," and his face would squinch up like I just released the most foul gas into the room. I was forced to admit that I couldn't lie to him. I had to be perfectly honest. Every time I would try to cover something up, he would give me that look, and I would, tremblingly, haltingly, expose my true thoughts to him. And he would respect them, even as he pointed out when my thoughts didn't take into account their negative consequences. He taught me to be vulnerable, to look inside at the worst of me.

In that time, I was forced to choose between my partner and my family. I was forced to acknowledge that I had a much older partner and face my thoughts of shame about being with a man I did not find physically attractive. I had to accept where I stood, and publicly take that stance.

It was a harsh mirror. I found myself unable to connect with my friends from college as my perspective shifted. But in that mirror, I discovered that I could see myself more clearly. I discovered I enjoyed being honest. I felt stronger, knowing that I couldn't lie without hurting others, hurting myself. The friends of convenience I had in college were replaced by friends of integrity. My "just a job" work was replaced by a career that respected open, honest communication.

This return to integrity led me to releasing the fears I hid from myself and hid within my body.

I didn't love my body. It was a machine that let me move about, not the orgasmic delight of sensation that it was meant to be. Steve suggested I look for a class on body awareness, and I found one through the local community outreach center. One of the instructors, Peter Hulit, was a massage therapist. During a break, I told him about my inability to feel my body. He hugged me, and was so strong and grounded, I broke down. I simply sobbed for no apparent reason while he held me.

I knew there was work to be done here.

Over the years that I worked with Peter, he taught me the value of listening to the body. As he kneaded a knot, emotion would tumble from the tensed muscles. Terror would leap from the knots along my spine. Anguish would pour from the muscles shielding my heart. Anger would erupt from my shoulders. My body had held these emotions because I was afraid to experience them directly, until I found someone who I felt would remain with me while I screamed, sobbed, and snarled. And when my body let go of the pain, fear, anger and sorrow, I became lighter, freer, more full of love. I learned that I could safely vent my emotions. I didn't need to hold onto them for fear of losing my mind. And letting go of them felt sublime.

I learned how joyful it is to awaken.

As I learned more about my body and let go of the larger, more enveloping emotions, I became aware of how the chakras relate to the body. I hadn't read any of Louise Hay's or Carolyn Myss' work, but I sensed that some of the ailments I experienced were connected to an imbalance in my chakras. I've used this as a point of exploration ever since.

I had mild hypothyroidism. After a year of elevated thyroid stimulating hormone levels, my endocrinologist wanted me to take synthetic hormones for the remainder of my life. Instead, I asked myself what relationship I had with my throat—my ability to express my truth. I slowly sensed a tightness in my throat. That tightness grew into fear. I was afraid of being physically hurt for speaking the truth.

This made no sense. My coworkers weren't going to physically assault me if I said something they didn't want to hear. If

I am faced with something that doesn't make sense, my answer is to walk into it, to discover why I think the irrational is rational.

So I signed up for a course on spiritual BDSM. I got the chance to experience pain in a safe environment. I got more than I ever expected.

Two men were flogging me. As my back was stung again and again, defiance suddenly surged within me. My face contorted, not in fear or anguish, but in outrage. I bellowed, "YOU CANNOT STOP ME! I AM RIGHT HERE!" again and again. I wrecked my throat for the next three days from screaming my defiance. The men working with me paused, and one of them asked, "Are you okay?"

My determination stabbed from my eyes as I rasped, "Keep going." He stepped back and went to work again.

When I saw my endocrinologist next, my thyroid was functioning normally.

What happened here? Where did this scream of defiance come from? When I told Steve about this experience, he sensed that I had been flogged to death in a monastery for breaking my vows of silence. I finally released what I was forbidden to proclaim then: I can express my truth without fear of dissolution.

Past life work figures heavily in my path. I don't look for past lives, but I don't discount what my heart says. If an image comes up from another time when I probe an emotion, I will follow it to whatever it wants me to discover about my release.

One time Peter was helping me explore sensation by strapping me to a bed, blindfolding me, and running a Wartenberg wheel across my chest. The small tiny prickling sensation, along with the restriction of my limbs, gave me the impression of being crucified in the rain. (Most crucifixions only involved tying the victim to a cross. Only the ones Rome *really* hated got nailed to it.) Suddenly a wave of despair washed over me. I cried, sobbing, "Why did you abandon me?!?" I felt like my friends had left me to die on this post.

The sobbing spent itself. In the vacuum, I felt the response, "We never left you. We were always by your side. You just couldn't see us. We were grateful that you did what you did. You will always have our gratitude."

My sobs of despair transformed to sobs of gratitude. I felt the love of my friends wash over me, tending to my weary soul and healing the wounds I bore for love. And I felt lighter.

Awakening means letting go.

We are meant to be open, loving creatures who feel light and joyful. Love is the very essence of our soul. It is only when our minds attach to past hurts that we gain emotional weight. So much of it happens in our childhoods, and gets reinforced growing up and in our adult lives, that we feel that life is a matter of climbing up a ladder with rocks upon our backs.

We find ourselves learning how to cope with the emotions we've bottled up, rather than releasing them. We bulk up on muscle —emotional armor, exercise—to make it easier to climb up the ladder, even though we weigh more with the extra load. But by releasing those emotions, that baggage, we get lighter, without needing that armor. As we let go of more and more, we eventually get to a point where we discover that, rather than climbing the ladder, we float up effortlessly.

Chapter 8

Steve almost lost his leg teaching me how to let go of resistance and live from my heart.

When he got a staph infection, we spent ten days in the hospital. I slept in a chair by his bed, doing what I could to buffer him from the nurses. I knew that, as sensitive as he was, and as comfortable with death as he was, I had to do everything I could to keep arrogant doctors and insensitive nurses from causing him to choose to die.

I suddenly felt my heart take over. Rather than feeling as if I lived from behind my eyeballs, I suddenly felt drawn from place to place, thought to thought, by a string attached to my sternum. I walked heart-first. My mind took a back seat while I was in the hospital.

In that space, it was easy to simply accept everything as it was. Steve realized that, even if he recovered, he wouldn't feel safe using the public transportation he loved. The steps onto the bus, the gaps at the train platform, the interminable standing at the bus stop, would be too much. He asked if he could get a car. I said "of course" without thinking. I didn't need to think. It made perfect sense, and the money meant nothing to my heart.

The three months of rehabilitation at home taught me what it meant to love through thick and thin. Steve was *not* a model patient. He hated being an invalid. Since I was not as sensitive as he, I was constantly overdoing things and getting in his way, adding to his frustration, and he was clear when he was frustrated.

Finally, after a month of absorbing his energy, I yelled at him for being upset. He was sitting on the couch. He paused, looked over to me, and gently said, "It isn't easy, is it?"

In an instant, I saw everything. I saw him in my position, tending for his former partner, who wasted away for 3 years during the initial HIV wave. I saw him completely understanding what I was going through. And, in that moment, I *knew* that he had done everything in his power to keep from exploding, every minute he was faced with his limitations.

And it was simply too much. He was in such pain and despair that, despite everything he could do, he couldn't keep it down. And he knew the toll it was taking on me, and understood completely that I couldn't keep down my emotions, either.

I burst into tears. And discovered that how I felt had nothing to do with love.

Love simply is. It's the subtext that underlies everything else.

Every emotion has love as its subtext. We are always in a state of loving. When we feel pain, we express it. If that expression isn't felt, it becomes hurt. If the hurt isn't recognized, it becomes anger. If the anger isn't recognized, it becomes apathy, then disconnection. Once we feel disconnected, we can cause harm without feeling the pain we cause.

But when love is focused on the pain, the hurt, the anger, the apathy, it all melts away, allowing the pain to be let go, returning us to love.

Steve passed away in 2008 from a stroke. His leaving was a shock, but he had prepared me well for it. I felt his presence with me for some time afterwards, and it was a comfort.

His passing is another story entirely. The lessons I learned after his passing is part of this story. Steve taught me what it meant

67

to be thoughtful and considerate, to read our hurts from the inconsistencies we tell ourselves, to heal them by exposing them to love.

My journey continued with several different players. Darcy Cleome, founder of the Amethyst Healing Center in Cambria, has taught me how to read and release energy that gets stuck within me. Aaron Base has been my brother on this journey, mirroring my challenges, and giving me the opportunity to learn from someone who is also learning.

Shannon Sosebee taught me more about love than any other person but Steve. I always thought "being in love with someone" meant that person "made" us feel loved. It felt disempowering to me, because that feeling of love was dependent upon the other person loving us back.

Shannon describes "being in love" as a state of being. She is always in love. When she meets someone else who is also in love, and they choose to be together, in love, then she speaks of being in love, with that person. But if that person leaves, she is still in love — just without that person.

That completely changed my ideas of relationship. It is not my responsibility to "make" someone love me, or someone to "make" me love them. We come together to share and enjoy each other's presence, not to complete each other.

Suddenly, every relationship became perfect, even if it didn't "work out." One relationship taught me about flirting online, another about flirting in person. A third taught me about allowing a person to be alright exactly as they are. A fourth taught me about my own self-esteem. Each of these relationships, while short, rounded out my idea of what it means to love someone without attachment, including myself. I can't help but love the experience.

I'm not yet finished with my awakening process. I know this because I still feel aches in my body where energy gets blocked. I still react to certain stimuli from fear. But I have the blueprint that helps me release the causes underneath this.

Appreciate what my body is saying.

Know that I can face my pain with love.

Let the emotion express itself fully.

Release the emotions and stories that surface.

Allow compassionate understanding to fill the space emptied of emotion.

Allow the gratitude for the compassion to release that blockage.

With this, I release my weights, allowing me to float up the ladder.

I am writing in a coffee shop in Riverside, California. I look around and see the low lighting in this vault-like brick interior; hear the indie music wafting from the speakers, the coffee grinder purring; smell the coffee and shelves full of old books.

I love the people inhabiting this space. The hipsters, punkers, emos, students, all living in their own worlds while touching each other's. Every moment is wonderful.

Chapter 8

Fifteen years ago I didn't see the people around me. I feared connecting with my heart, with others. And now, I see we always share our hearts as best as we can.

The world took me in.

Mine turned upside down.

And I am forever grateful for this experience.

Photo Credit: Michael Julian Berz

Lori Ann Lothian

chapter 9

Lori Ann Lothian

Bookends from God

"There are only two ways to live your life. One is as though nothing is a miracle. The other is as if everything is." ~ Albert Einstein.

I was nine years old when my first miracle happened. It was June, and a school field trip to the zoo was about to be cancelled in light of a monsoon-like morning. The torrential rain was forecast to continue well into the next day and yet I'd been looking forward to this outing for weeks. Like any good Aries, I wasn't going to take this lousy weather lying down. Home for lunch, I headed to the living room, pressed my hands together, knelt down and whispered, "Dear God, please stop the rain."

As soon as I returned to the kitchen, my mother (who had been washing dishes at the sink) declared she had just witnessed a glimpse of blue sky through the window. It was still pouring hard during lunch but by the time I finished eating the day had transformed into a hot sunny afternoon. And yes, by the time I returned to school, the field trip was back on.

Looking back, I realize this petition to a deity of weather management happened from that Zen space called beginner's mind. I wasn't raised to believe in God, but had heard from my devout grade five teacher that God was a miracle-worker who answered prayers. I simply believed him. This direct and immediate response to my request for a sunny day would become the springboard for a life of questing for the miraculous. At age nine, the mystic in me was born and along with it, the seeker.

It wasn't until age twenty-three that another episode of high-strangeness happened with the same dazzling force of the weather prayer. I'd already had a handful of mystical moments where nocturnal dreams came true, the most startling being a nightmare at age nineteen in which I was killed in an avalanche. I awoke to a breaking news story on my radio—an avalanche in the Alps had buried several skiers that morning. But these occasional precognitive dreams about world events remained a curiosity rather than a focus. I was having an experience but the experience was not particularly useful, nor repeatable. And it had little to do with me. That changed with a different kind of dream event, one that would alter my life trajectory radically, catapulting me from a tepid seeker into someone with a red-hot desire to understand the mind of God.

In 1985 I was a newly graduated journalist, diploma in hand, ready to tackle the world with my turbo charged enthusiasm and clever leads. But before launching into a fledgling career, I decided it was highly appropriate to backpack through Europe for several months. All my friends were doing it as a kind of rite of passage. The formula was to graduate from college and then enroll in the life of a euro-rail vagabond in pursuit of a degree in world beer varieties and youth hostel etiquette.

Just a few weeks before leaving on my three-month transatlantic adventure, a terminal pancreatic cancer diagnosis arrived that finally explained my grandmother's persistent back pain. This lithe and spirited seventy-seven year old was my mother's mother, the woman who had cared for me when I was an out-of-wedlock infant with a stressed-out mother, and to whom I had always felt a warm closeness—despite the perennial chill between my grandmother and mother.

My favorite and earliest memory of my grandmother was being snuggled into her lap on a wicker lawn chair late one night. I'd gotten up after a bad dream only to find both parents missing from their bed. Scared, I wandered downstairs to find my grandmother sitting in the living room reading a book. I'm pretty sure I was crying by the time she scooped me up in her arms and explained my mother's whereabouts—at the hospital to birth my sister. Instead of tucking me back into bed, she ushered us outside onto the porch, where we sat under the stars on a warm August night. I remember feeling safe and loved, nestled against her bony body. For some reason, perhaps because of that night I always called her Grandma despite her desire to be addressed as Grace. To me she was a "ma."

When I heard the cancer news, I was unable to absorb the terminal part and in heroic denial, tucked it away in the I'd-rather-not-hear-this part of my brain. I went off to Europe, promising my grandmother post cards (this was before email) to keep her updated about my travels.

Fast forward two months later: I've been beer drinking and sun tanning my way through a hot European fall, travelling mainly with one girlfriend from university but also in roaming international herds of post-college youth. In Venice my girlfriend and I bumped into a brat pack from Hollywood, one of them the now-deceased brother of Sean Penn. Back then Madonna was just dating future husband Sean, and so travelling with the "brother" was a glamorous thrill, one in which I envisioned myself writing an in-depth human interest story for a major newspaper, "Madonna's boyfriend's brother tells all." Or something like that. The point is, I was oblivious to my grandmother dying back home and instead completely absorbed by my own delusions of reportorial grandeur, not to mention Dionysian revelry.

October 24nd found me in a tiny pension in Seville, the fair city of oranges. The room I shared with my friend had two cots. Mine was the one beneath a window that did not close. I went to bed early, well before the usual tipsy collapse, because I'd been fending off a throat infection, picked up days before from swimming in the murky waters off of Tarragona, Spain. In fact, I was pretty sure I was feverish, though the chronic sunburn didn't help. (A northern Ontario girl in the Mediterranean does not produce a Coppertone tan.)

That night I dreamed of my grandmother. We were together in a kind of white haze of nowhere, though she was lying down and looked skeleton-thin. Her yellowish skin stretched taut over her cheeks the way animal skin looks on a hunter's trophy—too close to the bone and tissue-paper thin. She asked me, "How is your trip going? You forgot to send post cards."

I told her everything. I told her about the endless beaches, and the turquoise waters of the south of France, and the brush with the Hollywood crowd. Even about the ten days I spent sexing in Rome with a man I declared to her I would one day marry (and two years later, did). When I finished my travelogue, she stood up. "Look," she said, and before my eyes she began to change. Suddenly she was a young woman in her twenties, with radiant skin, flowing dark hair, piercing blue eyes and a broad smile.

"Grandma, you're pretty," I said in wonder. The grandmother I had known all my years had the deeply etched face of a gardener, lined by a life outdoors. That she had been beautiful in her youth had never occurred to me.

She gestured I should come close for a hug. She held me tightly and then dissolved just as I woke up to the sound of a bird squawking in the window over my cot. It was five a.m., dawn in Spain. I pulled my travel diary out from my nearby backpack and recorded the dream. I knew her hug was a goodbye. Somehow, I knew she had died.

For the rest of the trip, another six weeks, the dream haunted me. I suppose I could have called home (though expensive and technically challenging in those days). But instead I chose to deny the import of my experience and carry on as if it was just another dream. When I finally returned to Canada in late December, my mother picked me up at the bus station after a nine-hour ride from Toronto. The first thing I said was "Grandma's gone, isn't she?"

My mom nodded. "She passed away in October."

"October twenty-fifth?" I asked

"The twenty-fourth, actually."

I pondered this information for a few confused seconds before realizing I didn't necessarily have the wrong death date, but rather the wrong time zone. "Mom, what time exactly did she die?"

My mother paused to look at me like perhaps jet lag had rattled my brain along with my biological clock. "Around eleven at night. Why?"

I did the time zone math of plus six hours, which added up to my five a.m. wake up in Seville. "I dreamed she came to say goodbye to me. It was around dawn in Spain, a day later there. "

That night, as I drifted to sleep, I realized something else— she had not only come to say goodbye, she had come to teach me something. To illustrate plainly that time and space are no obstacles

76

to love. To give me a glimpse into the reality that we are not our bodies, and that we are connected to each other in ways I had never until then understood. Like my weather prayer, God was getting my attention. A deep yearning for Truth was planted in me. This seed would eventually become a magical beanstalk, a bigger-than-life mystical quest that would only really blossom in my late thirties—with the birth of my daughter and the death of my mother.

Getting pregnant was supposed to be easy. But now here I was thirty-six years old and trying everything to conceive, including inverse yoga postures post-coitus to make sure gravity helped sperm meet egg. Yet to no avail. After months of mid-cycle sex with my more-than-willing husband, it dawned on me that I just might not get that second child I'd bargained on. I'd waited nine years after the birth of my son, imagining I had all the time in the world.

After about a year of attempted pregnancy, I elected to see an energy healer called a polarity therapist, recommended to me by a friend who swore her bad knee was restored to perfect working order in only two sessions. I'd never been to any kind of alternative medical practitioner, but now desperation had crept up like choke-hold ivy. My doctor had let me know that the laboratory results showed my hormone concentrations were normal. This failure to conceive meant either one ovary was a dud or my husband's sperm were really bad swimmers or sparsely populated.

In the polarity therapy intake, I explained to a bespectacled grandmotherly woman in her sixties that conceiving a baby was turning out to be as tricky as winning at roulette. She nodded kindly, then explained her treatment in terms of balancing my yin and yang, along with releasing any buried emotions blocking the flow of "the breath of life." I almost added a sarcastic amen at that last part. But

Chapter 9

I wanted to believe in a cure for my fertility blockage more than I wanted to be snide.

"Do you truly want a baby?" she asked, lowering her clipboard and peering at me from behind owl-like wire glasses.

"Of course," I said, without hesitation.

"Sometimes we can be a house divided. Why do you want this baby? Don't answer me now. Just let the question grow into an answer."

I nodded compliance while my brain had already begun to search for an answer. Did I miss something in my own psyche, some buried fear of babies, or some inner conflict about childbirth other than the, oh by the way, medieval torture chamber pain?

As these thoughts raced, she instructed me to lie down fully clothed on the nearby massage table, close my eyes, and breathe deeply. While I did this, she silently touched my body in various places, in rocking, tugging and pressing motions. Her hands were gentle and in some way I could not quite define, nurturing. Soon I was drifting asleep into a dream in which my grandmother was holding me in her lap, softly humming a tune that was my mother's favorite song, one she had taught me as a child. "Que sera, sera, whatever will be, will be." I startled awake, to find tears streaming down my cheeks.

"It's okay," the therapist said. "Just sadness leaving the body."

I wiped my face with the back of my arm. "I'm not sad," I replied.

"The body is like a storage depot. It saves some emotions for when you are ready to feel them."

I sighed. If that were true, the only sadness I could imagine having saved for a rainy day would perhaps have been unspent tears at my grandmother's death twelve years earlier. Coming back from Europe weeks after she'd passed, having missed the funeral, I'd also missed a natural opportunity for mourning. It was as if I'd bypassed my grief.

"You'll get pregnant soon," the therapist declared as I left that day. "It was just an emotional blockage."

At once I realized the answer to her question, the why of my baby desire. I wanted to have a second child because I wanted to have a girl. I'd joked to friends that my order was placed with Baby Central for a pink blanket baby and I'd turn back anything with a penis. I'd already had nine years of raising a boy, and coming from a household of sisters, I missed the girl vibe in my home. But more than that, I missed the bond I'd had with my own mother, a connection that had been reduced to long distance phone calls when I'd moved to the U.S. with my husband a decade earlier. With a laugh, I realized I was not having a baby to do the classic save-a–failing-marriage-move, but rather, to find a new homegrown version of the love I had for my own mother, to regrow the mother-daughter bond from a new shoot.

As I drove home from that session, I found myself behind a car with a bumper sticker that read, "Grace happens." I laughed out loud. I'd just dreamed of my grandmother Grace and understood immediately this was a proverbial "sign" that something profound had just happened on the healer's table. God was trying to get my attention, again.

Sure enough, a month later, I missed my period. Nine months later, I gave birth to a girl. My first night in the hospital, exhausted from a ten-hour labor, I dreamed I was talking with my grandmother.

Chapter 9

This time, she looked old, just as she had before I left for my trip to Europe. At the end of the dream, she handed me something she'd had tucked into her arms all along—swaddled in pink, my baby girl landed gently in my own arms. I awoke in the darkened hospital room, my newborn sound asleep in the bassinet next to me. I didn't know what to make of the dream, exactly, but I had a distinct feeling that my grandmother was trying to tell me something.

It wasn't until a couple of weeks later, walking down the street with my daughter in the stroller, that the meaning of the dream became clear. A fellow neighbor spied us, and stopped to coo as most people do over freshly hatched people.

"She's just beautiful," the woman said predictably, even though clearly my girl was still a blotchy skinned, scrunch-faced newbie. What she said next, however, was far from predictable. "And Grace is such a pretty name."

"Her name is Hallie," I corrected.

"Oh, I'm sorry. For some reason I thought you named her Grace."

I looked at my brand new baby and remembered the dream of grandma Grace that first night in the hospital. I knew then. This child was my grandmother. She'd travelled far and wide in an afterlife adventure, sent no post cards, and in the end had come back to me. Life had a sense of perfect balance, a kind of cosmic bookends feature that in that moment, made me smile from ear to ear. Grace was back and I wondered—would she have dark flowing hair, radiant skin and piercing blue eyes just like the dream version of my grandmother the night she died? Was she showing me who she used to be, or who she would one day become?

My assertion that this baby was my grandmother recycled did not land well with my down-to-earth husband, a man so grounded in the mundane his roots surely went clear through to China. Yet one of the clues that my perception was not delusion came in the form of peppermints.

My grandmother had been addicted to peppermint. Yes peppermint in any form was her drug of choice, candies, peppermint patties (a chocolate covered mint candy) and gum. When Hallie, as early as eighteen months began grabbling for my Altoid brand peppermints (curiously strong, as the tin says), and sucking on them like sugar cubes, I knew this child was the latest edition of a woman who had held me in her lap when I was a baby. And later, when she developed a huge craving for stewed tomatoes (another of Grace's favorites), I had no doubt.

Nonetheless, it became painfully evident by the rolled eyes that few others in my intimate circle entertained the possibility of reincarnation, despite eastern wisdom traditions long acknowledging it as fact. A western scientist named Ian Stevenson had even dedicated decades to ferreting out almost irrefutable cases of children who remembered verifiable details of living as someone else. I know this because for a time I too was hell-bent on proving heaven was not a final destination but more like a waiting room between lifetimes. Then, one day I just stopped caring if anyone believed what I knew. The gift of knowing that my grandmother was doing an encore performance as my daughter was for me alone. This knowledge did not need to be shared to be any more potent a reminder of one simple truth. We are not mortal. We are eternal in nature.

Chapter 9

My mother lived with me the month before her own mother arrived on planet earth disguised as my daughter. The plan was to be on hand for the birth of the new baby, and to stay and to help out for a couple of weeks. Yet, Hallie was overdue by two weeks and by that time, my mother had air tickets home to Northern Ontario and obligations there as well. Later, when I realized that my baby girl was none other my mother's mother, it made perfect sense that the timing did not work out. The two of them never got along and just because Grace was now an infant, there were no guarantees the big chill would suddenly warm up.

Hallie was two years old when my mother died. (I could also phrase it this way: Grace was two years old when her daughter died.) It was not an expected departure on my mother's part, not one of those hanging out in death's waiting room with a cancer diagnosis and a morphine drip to the afterlife. After watching her own mother die a painful wasting death, my mom always said, "I'm not dying sick." She wasn't kidding.

The day my mother died, I awoke to a feeling of dread. I'd been stream-of-consciousness writing, a kind of "The Artist's Way" morning pages, although the content was more like a channeled metaphysical text than a purely creative rant. Mid-stream in the writing, these startling words appeared on the page: "Someone close to you is about to die suddenly. They will be healthy and will chose to leave from a place of strength."

I sat stunned in the coffee shop, dealing with this written warning by going over a mental check list of everyone I knew who might "choose to go out from a place of strength." I consider the most likely candidate my over-achieving World Bank husband, who I'd long pegged as a heart attack risk from work-induced high blood pressure. I briefly entertained my mother, but then crossed her off the list—she was simply far too dedicated a caregiver to my youngest sister who had been diagnosed with MS. My mother was, if anything, dutiful. And anyway, we had something like a psychic bond that surely would let me know she was in mortal peril—in fact only a few days earlier I found myself singing her favorite song from my childhood, Que Sera, in the shower. I called her up right after only to find that she too had been humming that very song the same morning. Over the years, I had gotten used to this kind of eerie coincidence when it came to my mother.

The day after the channeled warning my sky-is-falling feeling was so heavy it felt like gravity had doubled. It didn't help that 9-11 trade tower trauma had happened only three weeks earlier, and living on the outskirts of Washington DC, in the middle of an anthrax mail scare, made every day seem like doom's day. By 4:00 p.m., when it was time to pick up my son from school and daughter from her daycare, any hope my anxiety would lift had been abandoned. Instead I had a case of triple espresso jitters overlaid by dread.

I approached my car parked in the driveway in front of our riverfront house, surprised to find a heron sitting right in front of it. I'd often seen these graceful birds perched in the shallows, or sometimes at the end of our dock. But never in the yard, let alone in my driveway. It took starting the car to startle it enough to fly away. Deep in the back of my mind, I remembered that herons were considered in some traditions to be birds that ferried the souls of the dead to the afterlife. A chill ran up my spine, despite the heat of an Indian summer fall.

The call to tell me my mother had been killed in a pedestrian incident came that evening at 8:00 p.m., from my sobbing youngest

83

sister. Between the heron sighting and the shocking news, I'd gone shopping to buy my mother two birthday gifts. One a red sweater, and the other an owl statue, not knowing then owls too were considered portents of death. But I'd been so consumed with my life, especially in the wake of 9-11, I had only gotten around to purchasing her gifts a month past her actual birthday.

I remember two things about the night she died. I sat on the sofa in my living room, rocking back and forth, and mentally circling over the mystery of buying my mother's birthday gifts on her death day, as if this fact were a zen koan promising to deliver me from my shock-grief. And I remember this: Hallie gathering all of her stuffed animals around me in a plush circle of love. "It's okay Mommy, it's okay."

I had to laugh, even through my tears. Here was my two-year-old daughter comforting me as she did all those years ago, when she was an old woman and I was two years old in her lap on the porch on a warm August night. Bookends. God clearly loves bookends.

The weather on the day of my mother's funeral was overcast, a cold, dull grey day in early October. The service was held at a funeral home, in a room that looked like a miniature church, replete with wooden pews and stained glass windows. The minister spoke about God calling my mother home, and how even though her departure from life was unexpected (no one expects to get run over by a truck), there was a perfect timing in everything.

I too knew that her leaving was timed according to some pre-ordained schedule that surely made sense from a Gods-eye view. A week before her death, I dreamed I was sitting in a pew in a room fronted by a red and white cloth altar. Without knowing of my dream, my sisters had chosen to bury our mother's body dressed in a red sweater and white pants, one of her favorite outfits. Funny enough, the sweater was one she had purchased shopping with me when she'd visited at the tail end of my pregnancy with Hallie. And of course, on her death day I'd bought her another red sweater, one she would never have the chance to wear. The synchronicities were potently undeniable, God letting me know that all was as it should be.

Yet even though I knew a divine order was at work, I was angry. I was furious at the driver who ran over my petite five-foot mother. I was pissed off that I had not even talked to her once in the three weeks before she died, a rare stretch of phone silence that I could only regret. I felt such rage that I received a death warning the day before she died, that was utterly useless as prevention.

Though I didn't know it then, this anger would become a kind of rocket fuel that would propel me through a decade of soul searching, that would wake me up from my complacent domestic life, that would even contribute to the end of a marriage long stalled in the intimacy department. The little-girl seeker that had been launched with the weather prayer all those years ago, with the death of her mother, became a guided missile targeted at one question: Who am I? It wasn't enough to know that I was not this body, a lesson well learned by then. I wanted to know what the eternal truly meant. I wanted to know just how I was related to God.

I'd considered many names for my daughter and Grace was never one of them. The name I chose came to me in a dream when I was five months pregnant, a name I later discovered derives from halleluiah or, more colloquially, Praise the Lord. Another interpretation declared her name to mean "home ruler." Either would do: She was a bossy little Taurus bull, and she was also a constant reminder to me that "the Lord" works in mysterious ways.

Her middle name I chose as Alice, to honor the matriarch of my husband's family. Alice was a short, feisty Polish woman who survived the Nazi occupation and who loved to dance. She was not my husband's mother, but rather the woman who scooped up his divorced-then-widowed father and spent thirty years as his live-out girlfriend.

I loved Alice even when she scared me with her strong intuition and hold-nothing-back opinions. When I first met my husband, she told me in no uncertain terms, "You know that the twenty year age difference will be a problem for you one day." Of course, at twenty-five and madly in love with my new husband, she certainly wasn't preaching to the choir. She was right of course. Seventeen years later, when my husband retired and moved the family back to Vancouver, Canada she pointedly said to me, over lunch: "Your family is four horses going in different directions."

I knew exactly what she meant. My teenage son was mutating into a gangsta rapper who spent hours out of the house with his pot smoking buddies. Pre-school Hallie had retreated into cartoon TV, and my husband may as well have lived in Siberia instead of under the same roof for all the closeness between us. Two years later, we were divorced and both in new relationships.

The woman he took up with was thirty years younger and all predictions were for that unlikely union to fail. But Alice seemed to have a different take on things. "It will last as long as she will have him, and that's going to be for a lot longer time than you think," she told me once.

I really got to know Alice on the dance floor. It didn't matter that she was in her eighties, she couldn't keep those feet from tapping and her skirts from twirling whenever she heard a good beat. A performance folk dancer, she also came to nearly every one of my dance parties, and to more than one summer solstice dance bash held by my best friend each June. The last dance party before she died, she left early, tired from a daylong hike (her other love) in the mountains. She'd also been weary that whole year from a small stroke that had seemingly zapped the life force from her. Over lunch, tears in her eyes, she'd confessed to me. "I've lost my spark, and I don't know how to get it back."

I didn't have the heart to tell her that I didn't see her getting it back. The hundred watts called Alice had dimmed to forty, and in my mind she was in the waiting room to the afterlife. It was a matter of time before her name was called.

One day shortly after that lunch with Alice, I went for a jog after consoling a girlfriend whose depressed mother had called from Holland to say she wanted permission to end her life. As I set out on my run along the edge of the ocean, I stopped to sit on a bench that fronted a duck pond. I stopped because I had the feeling I needed to sit and just be still. Something about the conversation had left me rattled—was it okay to just choose to leave our bodies? Did we not at some level choose anyway; whether we chose death by car, suicide or cancer, did it really matter?

On the bench was a plaque, a memorial to a dead woman. Funny how many times I sat on these sorts of epitaph benches and never really stopped to read them. I finally got up to resume my jog, which took me over a footbridge spanning the duck pond. Just as I reached the middle, a heron swooped so close in front of me, I felt a breeze on my face. I ran straight home, not a jog but a sprint. I knew full well the heron's message. Someone close to me was about to die.

Chapter 9

Within minutes of arriving back at my house, my cell phone rang. It was my ex-husband's shaky voice with the news—earlier that day Alice had fallen on the street and hit her head, suffering extensive bleeding in her brain. They were at the hospital gathering her friends around her to say goodbye before removing life support.

That night, with my children gathered beside me, I kissed Alice gently on her cool forehead and told her how much I would miss her, but that I understood she was ready to leave. As she took her last breath, I held on to one sock-covered foot. She had small feet that loved to dance and had I closed my eyes, I could have imagined a child's foot in my hands. But I kept my eyes open and watched as Alice's own eyes opened just slightly, in the minutes before the attending doctor noted her heart had stopped beating. She'd been peeking I'm sure, not just at the crowd of those who loved her, but also at the destination—I'm certain this wise woman knew exactly where she was going next.

Three months later, early October, I decided to visit my sisters in my hometown, where I would also visit my mother's grave on the anniversary of her death. I didn't normally fall asleep in airplanes, but on this occasion I managed to doze off into a light sleep. The dream must have been all of two minutes long. In it dearly departed Alice told me a secret, her hand pressed against my ear. "I'm coming back," she said. "I'm due in May."

"And the mother?" I asked.

"Michelle, of course" she said with a giggle, as if this news was funny. I woke up with my head bumping against the cold window, and the flight attendant's announcement to buckle our seat belts for turbulence. Michelle was my ex-husband's girlfriend, the one thirty years his junior, that Alice had long predicted would stay the course. I knew she'd been struggling to conceive a child for at least a year and had even begun fertility treatments. It wasn't lost on me that her struggle to get pregnant had also been, like mine, at age 36. By now, I'd gotten used to the bookends phenomenon that life seemed fond of.

My sister picked me up at the airport two hours from our hometown and it was late afternoon when we made it back to the house of our growing up, a house she had taken over after our mother's death. The wall-to-wall living room carpet, where I had knelt to pray, was now the gleaming original birch floors. The sofa I had propped my elbows on to pray was still here, re-upholstered. Coming home to this house always had a bitter sweetness—it was filled with memories, from the times my mother was alive and in days after she died.

The living room, though, was the most saturated with recollections. It was the room of the weather prayer; the room where every Christmas we decorated the tree and opened gifts as children; it was even the room where my mother's ghost had answered a plea for help in finding her last will and testament. I'd flown in from the U.S. for my mother's funeral, to be followed that Monday by a reading of the will at the lawyer's office. My sisters however, had no idea where our mother had kept the will she'd drafted three years earlier after the death of our father. So my first night back in town, we all three headed over to our mother's house (just down the street from both sisters) to hunt for a legal document.

After two hours emptying drawers, cupboards and even looking under furniture, we'd all but given up. I decided to ask my mother for help. I sat alone on the living room carpet, tired and overwhelmed, and said aloud. "Mom, if you are watching over us, can you please give us a clue." I was thinking of all the times we'd had Easter egg hunts and she would give us hints by saying cold-cold or hot-hot depending on how close we were to the hiding spot. Within minutes of my petition for ghostly assistance, my sisters came thundering down the stairs, shrieking that the baseboard heater in our father's room had suddenly turned on even though the wall thermostat was in the off position. They were spooked by this, but I knew exactly what it meant--our mother was doing the hot-hot signal. Sure enough, we found the will wedged at the very back of our father's overstuffed filing cabinet. And as soon as it was recovered, the electric heat began to cool off, all without any help from a thermostat.

Now, a decade later, on the very day my mother died, I sat in this living room again remembering all the history that had passed through these walls. The late-day western sun slanted through the large bay window my mother had installed twenty years earlier, now decorated by my sister with candles and fairy statues. Caught in the crystalline wings of one fairy, the sunlight cast an arched rainbow right on the framed photo of our mother, a picture I had taken of her on her last visit to see me before Hallie was born. And though I knew it was just an optical effect, and that it must happen every day at this time, I couldn't help but shake the feeling that in the moment the rainbow was meant for me. All the searching and seeking for truth, was about to end.

On my return, I decided to gift Michelle a book on natural childbirth even though no one had yet mentioned that her year-long pregnancy attempts had succeeded. I knew better, because of course Alice had tipped me off. Sure enough, Michelle emailed a thank you note, along with the confession—yes, she was pregnant and just as in my dream, the baby was due in May.

In the meantime, something strange was happening to me. I noticed that life events bothered me less and less, and more and more nothing was ever wrong. Sure, I'd often talked myself into a state of equanimity in the past, with phrases like "everything happens for a reason," or every upset is a setup. But now there was no inner pep talk needed.

One night I dreamed a white haired woman guru kissed me on the forehead and said, "This is a full transmission." In the dream I opened my third eye and stared at what I knew to be the eye of god looking back at me. Another night I dreamed my heart exploded in light and I soared out of my body into the stars, following the call of an owl, until I reached an inky black pond that was oddly above me. I knew I was going to dive into that blackness and that it meant some kind of death. Another dream, I was on Ferris wheel, going 'round and round', and a voice whispered, "Die before you die."

I knew the dreams were pointing to either some kind of spiritual awakening or even a physical death. Because I'd long learned to trust my dreams, I took these messages to heart—I was either going to die or I was going to die to the self I thought I was.

Two weeks after returning from my visit to my mother's house, I went to sleep just before midnight. At 2:00 a.m., I woke up from a dream in which the voice of a spiritual teacher whose CDs I'd been listening to, said to me: "Lori, wake up. Walk the pathless path. Wake up."

I jolted awake, reached for my clock to check the time, knocked over my water glass, and laughed. My partner, asleep next to me, was now also awake, grumbling at all the noise. "I think I'm awake," I said, realizing that would seem to him like a statement of the obvious. I fell back asleep almost immediately.

Chapter 9

The next morning I looked at the world through new eyes and at first, it was as if everything around me, and everyone around me, had transformed into a source of delight. And then it dawned on me—the world had not changed; I had changed. Gone was the reactive emotional self, the distracted mental self, the arguing with reality self. Here instead was a vast, boundless joy and a bottomless stillness. And for once, I understood that the God I had prayed to all those years ago was none other than me. That there was only one of us here, one creative being in infinite forms, playing with reality and having an inordinate fondness for bookends.

The biggest bookend of all? The dream that started it all, the dream in which my grandmother said goodbye as she died, happened on the October 24th in Canada, October 25th in Spain. It was perfect then that I fell asleep on October 24th as Lori Ann and woke up October 25th as the very God that I'd been seeking all along.

* * *

Lori Ann Lothian is the creator of the popular The Awakened Dreamer blog which hit the stands following an overnight Enlightenment Episode that revolutionized her sex life and destroyed any chance at ever being miserable again. When she is not writing about self-realization, she's blogging weekly for elephant journal.com on enlightened love between the sexes. Lori Ann lives with her partner and daughter in Vancouver, Canada, where she has learned to transcend the rain and surrender to mega doses of vitamin D. Her web site can be found at www.theawakeneddreamer.com

chapter 10

Shanna MacLean (ShannaPra)

The Great Mesmerism and the Big Erasure

One day recently my soul sister, Yael, and I were sharing moments of some of the most powerful spiritual openings we had experienced in our lives. She remembered singing "Row, Row, Row Your Boat" as a child, and upon singing "Life is but a dream," saying to herself… "Yes! That's what it is!"

I remembered reading a channeled article years ago when I first began exploring spirituality. Two beings in the Light were comparing notes on their last incarnation on Earth. One said to the other, "You were absolutely stupendous as my mean father. I couldn't have believed you could get into such a role. I was scared to death of you." And the other said, "Ha, ha, ha… I was pretty good, wasn't I? But YOU, as the sniveling, cowering, powerless son… Now, THAT was a performance!" Hmm, I said to myself, "Yes! That's what it is!"

In the same light theatrical vein, here's a version of our drama as humanity, offered in Love—the way I have chosen to see our world. It has been completed in Spirit, but as we all know, it is still having a kind of re-run in the theater of Earth. We all love a happy ending, and why would there be anything else when Love and only Love is real?

Two Beings of Light meet as they travel through the Consciousness of All That Is. They stop to merge and have a (telepathic) conversation with one another.

Being of Light #1. Hey there! Is that really you? Wonderful to feel your energy signature again! You've been away. Weren't you visiting the place they call Earth?

Being of Light #2. Greetings, dear friend. Yes, it is I. Well, visiting is one word for it... Oh, yes. I was there in what they call a body during the Great Mesmerism and the Big Erasure that followed. My Twin stayed here at Home but he was always deeply connected with me. I was there for a long time in their way of counting time... It's so good to be Home.

Being of Light #1. How was it? What was it like? I've heard that many of our blessed brothers and sisters were trapped there in physical vehicles and forgot how to create. It must have been a tremendously frustrating situation.

Being of Light #2. Frustrating isn't the word for it! No one except our Beloved Creator is absolutely sure how it happened. It seems that it all started when some of our brothers and sisters thought they had been abandoned by our Beloved Creator. It was a simple misunderstanding. Do you remember, right after the Moment of

Creation, when God told us we were going to be on our own just a little bit... so we could begin to practice learning how to co-create?

Being of Light #1. I remember. It was very exciting, those first days of play, the first realizations of the amazing creative gifts we had been given. We were all joyfully experimenting. All those beautiful fruits and lush vegetation we made in the Garden of Eden...

Being of Light #2. Hmmm, not everyone found it so exciting. Being moved one degree away from the Ocean of Love so we could learn how to create on our own gave some of our dear brothers and sisters discomfort and the feeling that they had been abandoned by our Father/Mother. Of course, none of us had ever experienced individuation and even this tiny bit created confusion for them which led to a subsequent challenging situation.

You know how rapidly our thought forms materialize! Well, the distress of these souls brought on unusual feelings that they had never before experienced. On Earth there are words for those feelings: abandonment, rejection, loneliness, sadness, fear, helplessness and a lot of other things. Collectively these unsuspecting brothers and sisters were creating a big, dark energetic cloud that was beginning to move into form.

The idea underlying all of these feelings was that there could be something other than Love!

Being of Light #1. No!!! (pause) No!!! How could there ever be anything but Love? It's pretty hard to imagine what you are describing. What happened next?

Being of Light #2. Well, Love didn't stop, of course. It is who we are! But the belief that there **might** be something that was its opposite became really strong. That thought form—that there could

95

be something other than Love—promulgated all kinds of new and unusual possibilities and probabilities, including the idea that everything had an opposite. The word for this on Earth is "duality," meaning two sides to everything.

Being of Light #1. But didn't our precious bro's and sisters feel the Creator's Love and brush off these false feelings?

Being of Light #2. It became more serious than you think. Accompanying the effects of this collective creation was a great loss of faith and trust in our Creator. These false beliefs spread so rapidly that a special environment had to be created for these souls to live out their creations. We have always had free will, you know.

Being of Light #1. Of course!

Being of Light #2. The thoughts of fear—which is the name for the feeling that is the opposite of Love—were beginning to contaminate all consciousness. A special environment was finally created so that the dramas resulting could be lived out, and each soul could experience the results of its creations, as we always do. That was Earth. Our brother, Lucifer, volunteered to embody the whole experiment in his consciousness to provide it with shelter while it followed its natural course.

Being of Light #1. He has always been such a noble one and so dedicated to our Creator. His Love radiates far and wide.

Being of Light #2. So true. He really took on a massive task. But the biggest challenge of all for the souls on Earth was what they call the "ego."

Being of Light #1. I've not heard of that. What is it?

Being of Light #2. Indeed, it's not easy to explain. If I hadn't been on Earth, I don't think I would have believed it!

Do you remember that when we were given our co-creative gift at the Moment of Creation, God said we would not only have free will to create but a "mind" to help us in the organizational aspects of creating… to analyze how we were doing with our creations? It was meant to be a lovely tool to use as we created from the sensations of the heart and our inner knowing.

Well, this mind got complete control in our beloved brothers and sisters on Earth and became their guiding force. Our beautiful spirit family forgot that the heart—our intuition, our inner feeling—is the instrument by which we see, feel and KNOW. Even worse, they forgot who they are—cells in the heart of God with God's co-creative power. They began to think of themselves as helpless "humans"!

Being of Light #1. What a scene! Had anything like this ever happened before in Creation?

Being of Light #2. I'm not sure but I don't think so.

Being of Light #1. I did hear rumbles that the place called Earth was created as a holding tank to contain the random creating that was happening and to allow some brothers and sisters to play out possibilities and probabilities of their creating. How did you get there?

Being of Light #2. There was a call for beings who were willing to go there in service and assist. God wished for our precious brothers and sisters to release their distress and this false creation, and come Home. Many of us volunteered to enter Earth as if we were human, by the physical methods that had evolved the bodies or vehicles. We thought that we could hold the magnificent vibration of Home and help our siblings. On Earth we called ourselves LightWorkers and came to recognize each other by vibration.

Being of Light #1. When the Earthlings felt your hearts, of course, they changed their tune and headed back to God, right?

Being of Light #2. Oh, my dear, it wasn't that easy. The density in that creation on Earth was amazing. There was strong amnesia among the "humans." Most of them had forgotten God, our beloved Creator, completely and had lost their connection with Light and Love. They had also forgotten that our Beloved God was the Source of their life, their sustenance, their everything. Most of us temporarily lost our bearings and forgot who we were, too. We who had gone to help fell into the same traps of the ego. It took tremendous effort for us to regain our truth and to sustain it.

I call it the Great Mesmerism because the ego-mind constantly spoke within each person of the opposite of Love and created great fear and anxiety. Souls were mesmerized, hypnotized, and this created a consensual reality that kept feeding back on itself. It took awareness and choosing again and again to release the false identities that had been created and to hold a vibration of Love and only Love.

Being of Light #1. Wow! This is **very** hard to believe.

Being of Light #2. Well, as you know, God's Love prevails always and after a long period of what-they-called "time"...more and more of them started remembering our God and began connecting with Him/Her—meditating, feeling Home and losing their interest in being so human. This was a process and there were many stops and starts with each individual.

Our Beloved Father/Mother wanted them to make their own decision to return Home. Of course, our Creator was sending out the Love vibration very strongly and there were so many helping from this side as well.

Being of Light #1. This is absolutely fascinating. What happened next?

Being of Light #2. At some point the number of blessed souls on Earth who had opened their hearts and returned their trust to our Beloved Creator exceeded half of the population. This meant, in terms of resonance, that the majority wished to return Home. This precipitated the event I call the Big Erasure. It occurred at the end of the year numbered 2012 and it was beyond amazing!

Being of Light #1: 2-0-1-2? I know those are numbers and symbols. What did this mean?

Being of Light #2. Well, you know, dear one, how everything in Creation has both already happened and is happening every Now Moment. Well, on Earth one of the aspects of the drama being played out was something called "time." The concept of "time" became a very important part of life there. This was the false perception that one event followed another in a linear sequence instead of the "Now Moment" that we all know. The linear sequence was divided into blocks and given names and numbers. 2012 was one of these. They even measured their lives with a timeline and believed they "died," when after a certain point the physical vehicles they had created became old and tired. Oh, there is so much I could tell you…

Life there revolved around the past (things they thought had happened long ago of which they had memory); the present, what we would call NOW; and the future, what they imagined was coming. They often created "the future" on the basis of memories of the past, including "re-incarnating" back into bodies again and again at the end of lifetimes, only to experience the same problems over again. So there was much circular thinking and re-living the same kinds of experiences over and over, especially the unpleasant ones.

Being of Light #1. I am absolutely boggled! Stunned! I had no idea.

So are all of those beautiful cells of the Creator's heart back Home with us now?

Being of Light #2. Oh, yes. When more than half the souls on Earth had returned to the heart and reconnected with our Creator, an amazing gift was received, and this is what I call the Big Erasure. There was an explosive shift in the atmosphere, a great burst of higher vibrational energy, and the souls on Earth were relieved of all unpleasant memories of Earth life. All pain, fear, and the experiences they had lived that were less than pure Love were removed from their consciousness. In this way they were able to return quickly to resonance with Love and only Love, our birthright, and remember the truth of who they are. There was a brief period of reconciliation and readjustment of life on Earth to allow Love to prevail, but by resonance, we were then all returned to the consciousness of All That Is, our Home.

Being of Light #1. It seems you still remember some of your experiences. You are telling me about them.

Being of Light #2. Those of us who were helpers were perhaps less mesmerized than some of our brothers and sisters, and therefore experienced less erasure but all of us lost the feeling of fear which was the basis of the whole construct there.

Being of Light #1. Well, we are certainly happy to have all of you back Home. I look forward to greeting some of these souls and merging with them to feel more about this expanding experience.

Being of Light #2. It WAS an expanding experience. It seemed long and arduous when I was there but when I was lifted back Home, I realized that all of this had happened in a Now Moment.

When I intertwined here with some of the souls I knew on Earth, they were so ecstatically happy and renewed and so thrilled to be Home. The whole experience certainly stretched our consciousness! Now I truly know that our Creator is so powerful and so all inclusive that even the thought form that "God isn't" can be entertained!

Being of Light #1. You were brave to go to Earth and get into a "body." And you said your Twin stayed here?

Being of Light #2. Yes. One of us had to hold the vibration for the return and be a vibrational support for many during the experience. Holding the constant resonance of Home was critically important for those of us on Earth. My Beloved was very instrumental in guiding me and everyone with whom I came into contact—lifting us vibrationally when things got heavy.

I told him though…next time God asks for volunteers, we go as one being or it's his turn! I can't imagine we'll ever have something like the Great Mesmerism and the Big Erasure again, but who knows? Our fervent creativity and vast imagination know no bounds. We're Gods, aren't we?

Being of Light #1: Amen, sister!

* * *

Shanna MacLean (ShannaPra) was brought by God to Circle of Light in December 2001 to bring the Messages from God through Yael and Doug Powell out into the world. Before that meeting, another amazing reunion took place, truly an inter-dimensional Love story, between Shanna and her Twin Flame, Pra who is a Lightbearer on the other side of the bridge we are all building. Shanna has chronicled this Twin Flame reunion in her book, Eternal Twin Flame Love, The Story of ShannaPra. www.circleoflight.net

chapter 11

Kelly McCarty

Who am I anyway?

This relentless searching started when I was a little girl. My childhood was spent searching for the answer to this one persistent, lingering question.... Who am I really?

The cards, it seems, had been stacked.

I was adopted as a child and grew up without siblings in foreign countries where I was always in the minority. I barely knew my relatives and when we moved back to the states, I was thirteen years old and a foreigner in my own country. I didn't look or act like anybody in my adopted family who thought that I was overly emotional and way too sensitive. I had grown up overseas and was always an outsider, in one way or another.

This tendency, this urge, to figure out who I am, stayed with me, as the years went on, compelling me always to finally figure out, once and for all, the answer to the question, "Who am I?"

First, I looked toward numerology and astrology when I was an early teen. I would make endless lists of personality traits and favorites, trying to capture a definition of who I really was.

Then at the onset of puberty, I met what was to become my biggest guru. Suffering. Anxiety and depression combined with falling in love as a teenager in high school, hit me square in the stomach. Hard.

I twirled like any teenage girl, whirling around in circles, until I had spun a fairytale of a romantic love that could never die, I would never let it. I was not a complete person without this boy. My naïve, teenage mind told me that he was the only one for me, ever; he completed me for as long as we both should live. Soul mates.

He beat me up.

I fell apart.

Enter the '90s... therapy groups boomed, self helps books became number one best sellers, it was a carryover of the "me" generation of the '80s. Everybody, it seemed, was watching deep dark secrets and family traumas discussed on national TV to Phil Donahue and Oprah. Twelve-step programs sprouted up for every personal issue imaginable.

My self-reflective personality followed the trail of breadcrumbs from one author and teacher to another. Marianne Williamson, Deepak Chopra, John Bradshaw, Scott Peck, being among the most prominent. I didn't have a lot of furniture or clothes, but I had piles of books everywhere.

Then came the marriage. I've said it before and I'll say it again, nothing brings up the warts and blemishes of a so-called polished personality like a romantic relationship, especially when two people are as immature as my ex-husband and I were.

We fought, nonstop, for the full eight years of our marriage until our divorce. During that time I hit the darkest of lows, which at some points had me staring at the sharpest knives in the silverware drawer, wishing I knew how to properly use them, on myself. The threat of separation with him once even spurred a suicidal phone call which resulted in a stint in a hospital for the emotionally troubled.

I read many books throughout these troubled days. And finally something clicked. Maybe it was because I had circled the pattern too many times, for too long. My role had become well-worn and obvious.

I came across Eckhart Tolle's revolutionary book, "The Power of Now" and change began to take place.

I realized I had a craving for the intense pain I was suffering in my marriage's dizzying cycle of pleasure then pain. I had been repeating the same patterns without seeing the forest through the trees, which were constantly falling, in thunderous booms, around me.

And then one day I had had enough.

Before that, there was the story of shoving and screaming, the chipping of walls from items thrown at each other. There were epic stories of blame and the depths of despair and sharp echoes of the shouting and splatter of venom. And then, one day, he and I said goodbye.

Goodbye is free. Goodbye released me. The dream I'd been holding captive could fly up and away. The happily ever-after evaporated into clouds.

I thought I had wanted kids, a house in the suburbs in a nice cul-de-sac with friendly neighbors, weekend barbecues and being a stay-at-home mom. That's what I thought I wanted, until I was freed, released by goodbye. The change in my personality was noticed first by the people I worked with. They told me I was more bubbly, energetic, I talked more now, laughed louder. I was even called eccentric; I was called that more than once.

Chapter 11

I realized that true happiness for me, doesn't come from the typical formula that society lays out. I learned to accept the fact that I'm just not a traditional kind of girl.

I'm self-reflective, a bit nomadic, I care about ideas more than practicalities and I like to read and write, alone, for hours. I have more books than furniture, I let my cats have the bulk of the bed at night and I don't really care much, truth be told, for curtains, home décor or cooking meals.

I quit my office job and started personal training at a small neighborhood gym which quickly became my home. When I wasn't working, I was still there, exercising, socializing and making a home for myself. I knew every gym member by name and they knew me. They became my family. I developed girlish crushes on young men, men much younger than I was, and then went home and wrote fairy tale romances which never came to be.

I ate hope for breakfast and fantasy for dessert. I shrugged off every responsibility I could and spent all my time in the make-believe world I was creating in my head. In the meantime the clock was ticking. Tick, tick, tock. I could hear it in the background every so often, when jolted awake from a dream.

The carrot dangled and I kept grasping, not even frustrated by the game of it. But the problem with hope is that it whispers in your ear that the reality of now is not okay. Meanwhile life was still taking place while I was looking up at the stars.

Then came the whirlwind of events. The economy crashed like a tidal wave on the beach and the ripple effects ruined my personal training practice. Then came the onset of panic attacks and complacency and laziness. I was lifted up and away from my fantasy world and pushed toward the mirror. My face loomed large, unrecognizable, there was that question again. Who had I become? Who was I really?

I looked for myself in so many place, especially through the eyes of others; but while I longed for approval, I had chosen friends who were the least likely to ever provide it.

The beginning of the ending started last summer. I quit my job at the gym for a sales job which led to panic attacks. It was just hard for me to enter restaurants to chitchat and persuade people to buy food products from me. I'm an introvert. I couldn't handle the pressure. I crumbled. I quit the job. Enter the numbing sound of flat-line.

There I was, chasing others' approval and not getting it, feeling kicked in the gut time after time, not able to find work in a suffering economy and realizing from my spiritual readings that future goals and fantasies would not provide the relief to suffering that I desperately needed.

The anxiety I suffered was crippling. At this point I had isolated myself to just a few reserved friends. I had no desire to start new projects, write or grasp for the carrot . . . I was done with that, I could see the futility. Happiness was not to be found anymore through hoping my life away.

My depression was deep and physical. It made my skin hurt, my muscles ache, my chest throb. I thought about death often.

Many times before I'd asked the question to God, or to the Universe, or whomever, or nobody in particular . . . "Why, why, why am I here? Take me back," I'd plead. "I don't like it here anymore." I had days of crying and lying alone, staring at the wall, terrified.

There was nothing left to do but surrender. It felt as if the pain would rip me apart, but I did it. I felt the pain in my body, without labeling it. I allowed it, went into it completely, until there was nothing left, but sensation, and then there was no I left to do anything; it took me over.

At the eye of a hurricane, something amazing happens. The pain began threading apart, little by little, like yarn unraveling, or clouds spreading. It became a sort of energy, dissipating, gently and the ripples were quite lovely. A sense of relief washed over me, I had felt battered and beat up, but I'd made it through. The depression had lifted. For now.

I had pulled out old Eckhart Tolle tapes and after the lift of depression, randomly, I heard something I had never heard before. Eckhart Tolle asked a question, but in all the times I'd listened to that same tape, for years and years, somehow I had always skipped this part over. He asked, "Are you sure that the thoughts you are thinking are yours?"

Funny how something you've been listening to for years can one day open up, like a clearing of clouds in a stormy sky. Well, what did that mean exactly? I pondered it while driving and feeling frustrated in traffic. For years I tried stopping my "non-spiritual" thoughts as I tried to control my experiences. But with this new point of view, and probably as a result from my recent emotional surrender, I took a backseat and started paying attention to the thoughts as they came up. I wasn't doing them, "I" wasn't doing them, they were just happening, and the acceptance of that felt like a melting.

I'd be driving to work, sweating, because I live in Las Vegas and my car's air conditioning had decided, that summer, to die. I'd show up at job interviews with armpit stains . . . Couldn't be helped.

The traffic light would turn green, and when cars would leisurely move ahead, my thoughts would scream, "MOVE", the lack of wind in 105-degree heat was unbearable. But these thoughts weren't mine either. They happened on their own, and after they arose I started to accept the non-acceptance.

It was something I had heard, this time from Bentinho, a teacher I'd started listening to that summer. He said on one of his YouTube videos something about accepting the non-acceptance. As I contemplated this a prison began unlocking its doors inside my head.

Suddenly I understood what all the teachers had been saying all these years about no-self. Somehow, now I understood what they meant. I went back and reread and re-listened to old spiritual books and understood them completely differently now.

This brings us to now. Where am I now? Well, there's less striving and intensity, I can tell you that. There's experimentation now fueled by curiosity instead of desperation when it comes to the true nature of my perceptions, sensations and thoughts.

Jealousy, anger, mind reading, creating my own drama, obsessive thinking, all of that, still happens . . . . The habit of the me still seems so strong at times, and real. But there is a knowing that it's not real. I've looked for an entity called "me" and realized there was none to be found. The idea of "me" is just a tightly woven thread of thoughts which trigger strong emotions which perpetuate certain habits. But it's not personal and when a seeing-through happens, now, it's physically felt.

What good does defending something as precarious as a jumble of thoughts do? I don't think about the answer as much; now I look for it.

Chapter 11

Last summer I realized there was no controller at the wheel, and when the habit of controlling returns, it's let go of, more and more, in many ways.

So the story of awakening is apparently ongoing for this whomever, whatever I seem to be. But the desperate search for identity that marked so many of my childhood years has vanished. I'm satisfied with the paradox that I am nothing, not an entity, not anything that can be grasped, thought about or felt. Yet I am everything and was never abandoned or could be.

The little girl who once asked that question, all those years ago, only exists as thoughts, and thoughts are shape-shifty, snaky things, not to be depended on. I am the awareness that the memory of the little girl appears within, I am the timelessness of everything, that can't be located as a single I, and it disappears like the silence of the wind in the mountains. Who I am really is nothing at all.

William Martino

chapter 12

William Martino

Our Journey

Have you ever strolled through a scene in nature so beautiful that your senses are filled to overflowing? The whole body lavishly enjoys nature's nourishment. Enraptured in nature's bounty, a moment of transcendence occurs effortlessly, gently. It's this kind of experience that is reflected in our enlightenment traditions. What is the purpose of spirituality? Isn't it to improve ourselves and others?

We each have difficulties and hang-ups that might not be so easily understood by the other. In spirituality there is the common theme belief that "nothing's too hard to deal with." So, where do we start on the path of personal transformation—the common sense spiritual way?

Is it realistic for us to think that we can process all negativism and experience tremendous personal re-creation?

<u>Yes</u>

We each have the ability to transform apparent curses into blessings; negatives to positives. Are their limits to this action of self-inquiring transformation? No, I've never heard of a limitation as to how much love we can discover within our very own selves and how powerfully this love can affect us. Actually, the masters of life advise us that our potential is literally unlimited.

Can we really accept the statement that we are the stuff of stars, that Divinity is living within us asking us to be a vessel, to flow through us? The admonition to the child is you can be anything you want to. Do you and I still have this creative potential?

Our negatives can become positives. It's just the disciplined progression of personal metamorphosis that can be a bit tricky. We are asked to get concentrated and on-track right now. We do not always want to give up our nervousness; to let go and trust beyond what we can see. The funny thing is enlightened consciousness remains in us no matter what our choices. Unbounded love and power exist in us, forever, and we are sovereign in our ability to perceive it. In each mind, every emotion and body there is the pure energy that animates all life. It is this core thread of creation that emanates the impulse of life itself. One moment of this recognition is enough to heal a life completely. The sun and rain touch the lives of every person good or bad. In the same way our common inner Source is ever-present, willing to touch our lives if we allow. How about right now, right here?

What blocks us? Petty fears, concerns, demands . . . etc.

Forgiving yourself and forgiving the other(s) is the greatest act of self-empowerment that can be actualized. We are sovereign in our power of choice and we can choose being loving and furthermore, we can choose in each "time" to remain cultivating love through us.

Rather, we can allow love to cultivate through us. The body and mind are simply transfer units that bring spirit into form. When we are in this field of grace, all of a sudden we have enough space and support to see our way clearly. A new dawn rises in our consciousness and all is well. This kind of experience re-awakens our greatest dreams and belief in miracles; simple miracles, the kind that transforms who we are and how we live.

If we allow chaotic panic in any way, the pains of hell happen. When we stop, let go and trust, the pleasures of Heaven happen. Clearly intend which you're committed to manifesting in your life experience. Some may say "My mind is too chaotic; I just cannot quiet down, I have too many fears . . . etc." Each of us has the capacity to harmonize ourselves, whatever our situation. Physiologically speaking, there are over six trillion interactions going on during any given second. Each interaction is instantly known by all the other elements of interactions. Our minds and bodies are admittedly more complex than any known computer. We organize in ways that transcend the capabilities of all known machinery. Please contemplate the magnificence of your creation and inherent capacities. Have you got "it" in you? Of course you do. Smile, smile throughout every cell in your body; you are the greatest creation on planet Earth. Look around you, animals, insects, plants . . . you are the pinnacle of this worlds creation; that's quite a credit.

Sensitive scientific instruments measure the fact that the body, with all its electrical and magnetic movements, sings and pulses with wonderful sounds and colors on subtle levels of perception. The entire majesty of creation can be observed within. Have you perceived this or do externally oriented eyes, ears and psyche take all the attention away from you?

Stop it, drop it and grow roots here underneath you where you are. Let this be the consecrated place of your realization.

How can we make contact with the best within us?

Catalyzing our awareness into Spiritual consciousness we use a technique or series of techniques. Natural enlightenment suggests that your religion is made up of the beliefs, practices, visions, words, etc., that work for you as an individual. As we awaken our presence undergoes a dramatic transformation. We appear brighter to people; the whole world appears brighter to us. The masters of life have a living presence which emanates tremendous power. I invite you to explore people like Ammachi, Thich Nhat Hahn, The Dalai Lama, Ramana Maharshi, Satya Sai Baba, Eckhart Tolle, Carolyn Myss, Deepak Chopra, and Wayne Dyer. These people and many others actually are pointing toward the missing link for mankind. No longer be isolated without the help of others. There are so many people that actually want to just help, out of their abundance. We all could use a little help, couldn't we?

I've found a very curious phenomenon in my life I'd like to share with you. Each time I actually accomplish the inner work of actually changing and behaving better, opportunities seem be created out of thin air.

The Invitation

The invitation is for you and I to recognize that life is present for us here in this moment. No waiting for some other moment. Now is the best time there is to accept the full measure of Divine grace, protection and providence into us . . . completely throughout. As a miraculous touch is given by a loving hand, in the same way embrace pure Spirit into your heart and know the truth of "born again." The opinions of others during this process must be carefully observed because we are all too often negatively affected by the doubt others possess. If it is your doubt then repent; if it is just the other's doubt, have mercy. The quality of our circumstances, all these transitory experiences come from the spiritual. We learn to focus on the feeling we are maintaining, and in that we can see the creations we are making in our lives. Let the appearances of things go and know what you feel instead. In this sensing mode we can find our way to the spiritual transformation that touches every aspect of who we are and how we are living. Do you want to make great strides in your life? Let go; let go of me, you, him, her, they, that, this . . . Take a breather. Learn who you are first through infusing your simple daily life with the newfound vigor of Spirit. Do you know the art of "getting Spirit," being in "good spirits," "inspired," etc? Learn this art with The Healing Alliance as your friends.

Our focus must be in the unchangeable nature of our inner existence. Beyond time, space and circumstance we are invited to be established in ourselves; it is only within the self that we can find God, the spiritual and pure energy and elements. Now, where will you be looking today? Not just our own Self, but the inner self and truth of all people, animals, and nature, even matter. The unified field of energy is the field from which the matrix of creation is born. Identify with that, with nature and progressively make your way to spiritual perception; the most subtle level. What joy power builds inside us?

"All I know is all I feel right now, I feel a power growing in my hair." ~ Cat Stevens

Why is it that all of the enlightenment pathways talk about an incredible ecstasy that comes along with spiritual maturity? The texts and "masters" clearly share with us that intense love, joy, bliss, ecstasy "is" the power that changes lives and creates miracles.

You and I herald much where we walk. Think of how many individuals are touched by your life every day. There is some kind of "energy exchange" going on right now between you and all mankind. What are you putting out? What kind of legacy are you leaving for the world?

How will we accomplish being kind with each other? Miracles are realities and they can continue happening to us if we just take the time to stop and tune in. Is now an okay time to secure the healing of your life?

The Divine inoculation is received purely as a matter of choice. There is no preparation or practice necessary. Faithing means to believe and generate the Spiritual energy necessary to accomplish the moment. One moment, just one moment of sincere practice, begins the process of self-discovery. No longer do as the others, no longer be attached to whether or not people like or respect you. Fly through life free, internally soaring free as the eagle, having your own principles clearly defined in your own heart and your clear sense of purpose guiding your way forward. You know what you want; you want love, and you know where you are headed, into love's fulfillment. Love is far greater a power than the ordinary person understands. When I say love I'm not speaking only of sentimentality; rather I'm speaking of the tremendous creative force that binds life together.

Infuse Your Life

Have you ever felt a change in atmosphere during some exhilarating moment? The very air within and around our bodies has a different feel to it.

Interestingly, the origin of the word Spirit is air and breath. We hear reports of yogis and all sorts of masters experiencing inner winds, waters, oils and fires. Have you ever felt an inner healing, feeling that has the sense of warmth and magnetism to it? Let's take a moment to initiate the manifestations of Spirit's Presence right now as you read this article. Willingness is the only necessity. Remember a time when you felt loved, accepted, secure and nourished; any of the positive emotions. Can you feel it? If not, why not? Let's bring grace here with 120 seconds of pure bliss . . . time off from the concerns of life as we enjoy breathing deeply and fully; thoroughly release pent-up stress. Sigh loudly in the expulsion of your grief.

Travel into your pain and release it; again, again . . . . Taking time for the releasing of your very self is very worth the necessary investment of time and energy. Worry about no-thing; return to the place where "things" are after-the-fact. Be as spacious as space itself.

Is there a change of atmosphere in your space that you feel within and around your body? Even in the least degree? Can you feel the Spirit? There seems to be confusion in some circles as to whether we should feel or not. Of course we should feel! Do you think the intellect is greater than feeling? Discover Love, Spirit, pure energy, nature's elements and deep relaxation . . . These feelings combined make "magic pie."

These are the feelings that reveal where we are in fear, distorted and/or out of balance. There may be some elements that are difficult to face. This is what purification is all about. Purification and confession are the same thing. Once we admit to what is, what has been and what should be, we are automatically coordinated into proper alignment. We may rather like to hide in fearful clinging rather than be revealed as imperfect and have to be re-shaped. For some, it's just too much to look at the truth about themselves. However, I humbly submit that though we may be apparently flawed, what's beneath that is an unshaken core that knows the majesty of life. If we are to bring this forward, just for a moment, transformation begins occurring quite naturally. No effort; we change because we are inspired to do so. The painful elements of our self-awareness become enveloped by so much support that we are encouraged to face ourselves and morph into a better version. A few downloaded upgrades will do just fine. In this way evolution is insured.

"Then said Almitra, Speak to us of Love. And he raised his head and looked upon the people, and there fell stillness upon them. And with a great voice he said: When love beckons you, follow him, though his ways are hard and steep. If in your fear you would seek only love's peace and love's pleasure, then it is better for you that you cover your nakedness and pass out of love's threshing-floor, Into the season-less world where you shall laugh, but not all of your laughter, and weep, but not all of your tears. Love gives naught but itself and takes naught but from itself. Love possesses not nor would it be possessed." ~ Kahlil Gibran, *The Prophet*

Samadhi Consciousness

"In the state of Samadhi, all one's different kinds of energies come under one's control. It is not blankness or darkness of the mind. When form is ignored and meaning alone is felt, that is Samadhi. When the person engaged in meditation forgets both himself and the fact that he is engaged in meditation, and then it becomes Samadhi. Samadhi means the fixing of the mind, free from all impulses and agitations, on the Lord or on one's own Reality. It indicates the state in which one is in one's own real nature. Samadhi is when one is free from all duality. The mind will be unshaken by dual experiences; it will shine like a flame in a windless room. It is unmoved and unmovable." Sanathana Sarathi, August 1989.

Samadhi is the pinnacle of spiritual accomplishment in spiritual practices. This is not a skill that is restricted to sages. We all experience this all empowering state of mind quite regularly. Each night when we go to sleep, we do return to the place where there are no problems, nor could there ever be. What's the difference between this moment and the moment of blissful nourishment found in the deep sleep we experience every night? It's only a state of mind.

Prayer

Prayer leads to meditation and meditation to Samadhi. Prayer is simply communicating with someone else for advice and intercession. We cannot figure life out without asking for guidance. Prayer is perfectly logical. What kind of prayer we do is up to our individual preferences. Meditation practice as given us by the saints always finds its way to this Samadhi experience. Samadhi means "being in and from that disappeared place caused by the rapturous buildup of the miracle streams (Light, Silence, Current, Sound, Love, Joy, Bliss, Contentment, etc.). In the Hindu, Buddhist and Taoist teachings this is where enlightenment is granted. Whatever spiritual tool we apply, it is in Samadhi-consciousness where we are freed. We should know then when our techniques are done properly profound peace of mind, emotional transformation, deep relaxation all happens.

How to Use Spiritual Techniques

Our techniques are like the space shuttle on the back of a plane. The plane is all our techniques and we are the space shuttle. These two must function together perfectly. When the plane's assistance is no longer needed, we enter unbounded space and are liberated to restore ourselves fully. Creating this experience for ourselves daily, and then bringing it to and through our lives, is the Divine blessing meted out to every man and every woman. Will you graciously accept your dispensation today?

Sharing with Others

Each person has some measure of compassion for the whole. We are, in effect, all in Love with each other. Think about it. Do you have compassion for all mankind? Of course you do; each person knows universal compassion. Only some take the action necessary to consciously realize it. No time, space, urgency, need; be in the abundance that is ever lavishly flowing. All fleeting things have vanished from the screen of awareness; only the eternal elements remain. All satisfying experiences naturally flow to us when we are "in the right place at the right time."

Here is the Right Place, Now is the Right Time

Enlightened (Samadhi) consciousness in no way leads to flightiness, escapism nor grandiosity. Rather, it's with this kind of beautiful "vibe" that man is remade and charged with the breath of the Divine. Do you want to be re-made? Would you like a new lease on life? Do you need an energy infusion? All these blessings continually flow from enlightened consciousness. Union herein deposits the power to make changes happen. Great and positive actions naturally flow from such an empowered one. If you release the "outer" and refine the "inner" then the "outer" will be able to accomplish what you seek. We must not compulsively search for external solutions to internal problems.

If the only real blockage to your success is you, I suggest that is where you focus. Releasing the "outer" can be scary, but just do it anyway. Travel further and further into pure Spirit, Nature, Cosmos, Energy, Consciousness, Habit . . . Find and implement the Divine aspects of each of these and watch the miracles unfold in your life.

Do you see now why releasing the outer is so important? It's because we are all compulsively bound to the outer external appearance of things. To solve this external dualistic addiction we must ingest the medicine of Spirit, Nature, etc. We today discover free access to greater thresholds of "the qualities of pure consciousness."

The way this happens is, first for a flash of time we experience a moment of unbounded-ness and release; then we again become distracted. Our practice is to extend these flashes into moments, and moments into minutes, and minutes into hours in retreat/intensive situations.

Stretching, shaping and releasing into the experience of anointing are the keys to higher personal development. With time and practice we are awakened to the fact of being connected to inexhaustible resources.

This is all quite scientifically supported. It's this type of profound restoration that is responsible for creating the better life we all seek.

Living Heaven on Earth

This is where the spiritual rubber meets the physical road. The moment is our application ground for spirituality. Ordinary relationships, common duties; this is the stuff of our lives. Each day, with every series of events, is opportunity. Opportunity to demonstrate what we believe in.

If it's not our families, the grocer and the gas station attendant, then where else will we go that takes greater importance? If not the neighbor or the mailman and all those in our lives, then who shall we demonstrate love with? Love is an action word. Yet it's an undoing that we do. We are brought up, virtually all of us, with a set of relational instructions that could use the master's touch. We're educated in boundary setting and assertiveness, etc. The entire world society/relational paradigm is built on an unenlightened structure.

Being spiritual pioneers in our daily lives is ushering in a new and better world for our children and our children's children. We mustn't be depressed nor self-isolated. Smell the air; let the sun, sky and universe in. We all walk together as one great soul discovering itself. Once we are simply overflowing with good energy, we naturally want to share, and it's in the simple things that such great energy is best invested.

Servanthood is the crown of human achievement. What greater joy then to bring a smile to someone's heart? With each environment we enter "servicing" the sparks, the rapport necessary to connect with others. Simply lending a helping hand brings so much joy to our world. There are no valid opposing reasons to this practice. If all the Saints and Sages were gathered around here (which they are, of course), we would be assured that healthy spirituality is a good thing to actualize in our daily lives.

We mustn't wait for something mystical to happen to have more faith; rather, have more faith first.

"Our deepest fear is not that we are inadequate. Our deepest fear is that we are powerful beyond measure. It is our light, not our darkness that most frightens us. We ask ourselves, who am I to be brilliant, gorgeous, talented, and fabulous? Actually, who are you not to be? You are a child of God. Your playing small doesn't serve the world. There is nothing enlightened about shrinking so that other people won't feel insecure around you. We were born to make manifest the glory of God that is within us. It's not just in some of us; it's in everyone. And when we let our own light shine, we

unconsciously give other people permission to do the same. As we are liberated from our own fear, our presence automatically liberates others." ~ Marianne Williamson

Until we meet again together, we have explored Heaven's offering of meditation and its true source as Spirit in the moment of life. The worst of all problems shall pass. Do not worry; grace has brushed the canvas of our lives before and it will do so again and again, until our evolution is complete.

I leave our time together with warmth in my heart and a glint in my eye.

* * *

William Martino is the author of *SPIRIT TOUCH: The Masteries In Meditation.* He can be found at www.WilliamMartino.com

chapter 13

Mystic Life

From Logical Atheist to Nonlinear Mystic

I had it all figured out from a young age. Science *proved* that there was no purpose to any of this whole life thing. Some chemical reactions had occurred millions of years ago, followed by eons of mutations, which eventually lead to our ultimately meaningless existence. Here we are, I thought . . . so what?

To add to my sense of certainty I would occasionally watch glimpses of televangelists asking for money from their confused and desperate masses. It only increased my cynicism that there was anything whatsoever to spirituality. We were here for an average of seventy years, and would vanish into non-existence with no memories, no awareness.

To avoid my underlying existential dread I would distract myself constantly. To peer into the abyss of death was too much, so I'd selfishly cheat on partners, having affairs to find brief escapes from the dreary pain of life. I would sneer at anything spiritual and think that it was nothing more than naïve delusions to avoid the fear of death (not recognizing how much of my own life was about avoiding *my* fear of death!).

Nevertheless there was something small within me that yearned for meaning. Around the age of nineteen I read *Siddhartha* by Herman Hesse and enjoyed it greatly. I wasn't near considering myself an adherent to Buddhism or any form of religion, but the suppressed spirit within me said, "Hmm . . . this is interesting."

Some years later I found myself exploring the *Tao Te Ching*. It seemed as though spiritual text that didn't mention the word God could be at least somewhat palpable. My mind was full of too many negative associations with the word "God" to ever find such a concept appealing, until the age of thirty when I read the *Conversations with God* trilogy by Neale Donald Walsch. It had been recommended by a friend whose opinion I trusted, and I found it extremely appealing. It opened my heart, and my mind. Around the same time I had begun using divination sources such as *Osho Zen Tarot* and the *I Ching*. Synchronicity began to powerfully blow the lid off of my logical mind, and I soon realized that there was much more going on in the world (and beyond the world) than linear "logic" could explain!

I was eventually guided to write about spirituality, and have written five books and dozens of articles in an attempt to put into words the perceptions that were becoming clear to me. I could see that there was a spiritual realm, and it was speaking to me with increasing consistency as I learned how to listen.

I became drawn to the tradition of mysticism which I learned was direct communication with God instead of receiving teachings from a priest or other "authority." I was guided to a "pen name" to reflect my new self . . . and became Mystic Life. Impending death became replaced with an interest in physical immortality. Affairs became replaced with an interest in polyamory as a way to honestly love more than one person. And beneath these earthly concerns grew an understanding that a peaceful mind was my ultimate goal. I came to believe that the one guiding principle that I would embrace when making choices was the ongoing question, "Will this bring me greater peace?"

Now, as I help others on their path as a guide, or as a friend, I have empathy for wherever they are. I've experienced many extremes throughout this life, and the benefit of having been a devout atheist is that I can compassionately relate to the religion of logic. I know that until someone is ready to open their mind to the spiritual realm, they will most likely not experience it . . . and life will make perfect sense. However, I believe that an ever-increasing number of people are awakening to new possibilities, and I feel that my journey is grounded in the knowledge that everything I've experienced has elegantly manifested to help me assist others as they awaken into a meaningful, spiritual life.

* *

Mystic Life is an author on personal and spiritual growth who enjoys sharing ideas from spirituality and psychology that increase well-being. His books and videos can be found at www.Unification.com

chapter 14

Trip Overholt

You, the so-called "person" reading this page on your iPad, computer, notebook or Kindle—you are reading from one of two possible outlooks. If you are like I was until the age of 48, you believe you are an individual person with a brain that is the seat of your awareness.

You believe yourself to be a doer of things, the I-thought with free will, and that you have some control over the outcome of your game of life. You believe you exclusively exist in a particular location at a particular time and that there is a world "out there" full of objects that exist independently from you and from each other. This is a dual outlook.

There is also the outlook of non-duality. Anyone can taste enlightenment anytime by asking the question in the very *Now*, "Who or what am I?" The truthful answer always is, for everyone, the same still silence that avails itself as this I-thought vanishes or becomes transparent. So the Truth is we are literally nothing. Inside of that no-thing everything mysteriously appears like a movie on a screen.

That contradiction of simultaneous something AND nothing cannot be grocked by the mind. It can only be intuited by grace. The mind can point to it with lots of juicy words but it can never know or own it for itself because the mind is not external to it. It is within it. Something cannot know that which contains it. It can only BE it. It is all so maddeningly simple and so profoundly ever-present as to be beyond detection.

If you had to pick the biological organ that has the greatest impact on your well-being you would probably say "my brain". If someone were to ask you who you are, a voice in your head would say, "I am so and so, a mother of two children, who is married and works at such and such". In essence, that voice in your head, the "I-thought" is the sum total of everything you have ever known, felt, or experienced and who you think you are as a story line. And when your body dies, that "I-thought" or "narrator" in the form of a "personal soul", will depart your body and go on to abide for "eternity" in one of several possible suspect locations.

A spontaneous transformation or dispensation of grace in human consciousness seems to be taking place in the information age and emerging as the Truth of what we really are as *Now.* It is at the very fingertips of much of humanity. I am a living example of that phenomenon. Many of you have had the taste and are affirming that. Reading these words is not an accident. It is an affirmation by the same grace.

All of that sounds like a bunch of words and of course, it is. Word symbols cannot prove anything or transmit anything to anyone. If, upon their reading, an apparent spiritual transformation takes place in a reader, it is because the reader is ripe, with a mind that is empty enough to embrace a radical new "over-standing". Ironically, it has little to do with the "worthiness" of the one so blessed.

Unbeknownst to me, I was in such a state of ripeness when I walked through the Wizard's bedroom in 2006 and caught a glimpse of an open picture table book with large type lying on a side table in the bedroom. It contained quotes and pictures of the venerated Indian sage, Bhagavan Sri Ramana Maharshi. I stopped and read a line or two. I flipped the page and read another. Three or four pages into it I had a full blown meltdown.

Tears streamed down my face. The knot in my solar plexus (that had been there for so long without even being noticed) unclenched. I suddenly, irrevocably realized I was not a separate individual with a personal consciousness that "belonged" to me (residing between my ears) but rather, an underlying awareness that was now somehow perceivable. I had been blessed by grace with an awakening I was not even looking for. In that moment there was joy, grief and relief. I realized that eternity is here and *Now;* a deathless reality. What joy!

But to experience that Truth, I had died to myself as a "real" i.e. "separate" person that should be taken seriously. All of my prior striving for happiness, primarily through my relationships with women, I realized had been completely unnecessary. And with that realization, a huge burden was lifted. There was nothing I needed to do, learn or gain. I had come home to my Self. I intuited or perhaps better said—had the "felt sense" of the immense sanctuary that is nothingness.

Chapter 14

As the tears of ecstasy and grief literally flowed down my face, I could immediately sense that a veil of illusion that kept me out of the flow of life was lifted. For the first time, there was tacit realization that the seat of awareness was not between my ears but rather infused my physical form which merely borrowed its sentience from "that" ocean of sentience. Simple Being was awareness itself—timeless, formless and without beginning or end. I was, for lack of an even more exuberant description (I would use if I had it), "God" itself, an impersonal, nameless, eternal reality.

Curiously, tears of grief streamed down as well—as though I were attending the funeral of my very best friend—and that friend was me, Trip. That beautiful man who had tried so valiantly to always do the right thing, who had suffered so much despite his noble intentions, that beautiful man was mortally wounded. I would like to say dead but that has taken some time.

Crucially, in that very moment, the arch of my life shifted from one of doing to one of Being. With that paradigm shift has come a causeless, priceless joy that inhabits the headless heart any time it is given attention. This resplendent joy is available to anyone regardless of their station in life, intellect, or physical condition.

Why, once exposed, some go on to investigate this possibility and others do not, is a great Mystery. In my case, the clean simple words of wisdom expressed by Ramana Maharshi exquisitely mirrored my Self. For that I am eternally grateful. And while I do venerate Ramana Maharshi as the ultimate example of what an ordinary man can be, I do not worship or deify him. We are equals. He is a mirror of my true Self.

What happened to me is extraordinary only by the smallest of degrees. All of us have shared a similar taste. Some get it on psychedelic drugs or through near death experiences or by being "in the zone" or in moments of breathtaking exhilaration or in Satsang with a true teacher or every night in dreamless sleep. What makes the pivotal spiritual experience unique is that it "sticks". We simply reach a point of ripeness where we are ready to surrender our individuated personhood for the joy of Being.

As powerful as my experience was, it was too incredible to be believed. My mind could not contain it. No death!? God is everywhere and this is heaven? There is no time or space, just simple Being? To own all of that through my heart as direct experience unsheathed by thoughts requires a still mind. And that would require the answering of my many doubts and questions by an established mentor or sage. For my path, as it turned out, was that of wisdom, Jnani, and my brain was not going to take a knee to my heart on the strength of a teaching, a guru, or God itself without the satisfaction of every last answer to every conceivable question. For the next five years I would be blessed with a spiritual enlightening sojourn of supreme quality that unfolded without having to lift a finger. This is the nature of grace. So beautiful!

Immediately following my spiritual experience, my friend, John Troy, aka "The Wizard," emerged as my spiritual pal and mentor who had already been my friend for fifteen years! I had not had "the ears to hear" what he'd been sharing all along, and he, in his wisdom, had not pushed any teaching on me. He simply shared freely with me.

At this point, no pushing was required. If you have seen the movie "The Matrix" where the main character is strapped in a chair and absorbing life threatening doses of downloaded kung fu expertise through direct stimulation of his brain, you might appreciate the comment, "he's a machine". With the possibility of heaven on earth at hand, I paid attention to the answers to my every

133

question as though my life depended on it—and not just once. I recognized that assimilation of Truth would take time, and would need to penetrate to the core. This would require attention to repetition and so I listened with rapt attention to the same answer one hundred times. I yearned to own lock, stock and barrel, every shred of Wisdom and experience contained within the corporeal form of my teacher. Wouldn't you if immortality and heaven on earth were the payoff? That yearning was so intense that it quickly drew to me the grand-nephew of Ramana Maharshi for additional affirmation.

As a grand nephew, V. Ganesan had been raised near Ramana Maharshi himself, had graduate with a degree in philosophy, spent a lifetime caring for the old devotees of his great uncle and time with modern sages, and had an encyclopaedic knowledge of spiritual nomenclature he was happy to download into me on a silver platter. I sucked it up like a drowning man sucks for air. Now, not only had I the direct wisdom of my wizard mentor, but also the wisdom of the ages as accurately recollected by this second skilful teacher, who would say, "here is what Christ said about your question," and "here is what Buddha said," and "here is what Ramana said" and "here is what the Japanese grand Zen master I met in 1957 said." And not only that, but I was given the behind-the-scenes look into Ramana Maharshi's ordinary life, the never-before shared stories of compassion and transformation that took place between the venerated master and those in his company, some of whom were animals!

Taking a breather from my spiritual tutoring and from a day job as a real estate developer, I took up my long-lost friend's invitation to attend the epic artists' festival in the desert known as *Burningman*. This looked like a serious event, with harsh conditions in the middle of nowhere, with a challenge and opportunity to recreate myself any way that I desired. I was called to conduct an experiment in unconditional love. The moment I hit the ground, I was to assume my own divinity and the divinity of everyone I met— not as a concept but as an already accomplished fact. Furthermore, I would assume that everyone that I met was worthy of unconditional love, without resorting to the instantaneous judgments and reciprocity that had been my habit based on initial appearances. I was able to be both of those truths wall-to-wall throughout what turned out to be one of the most mind-blowing events of my life, and I lived on a cloud for two months afterward. While the magic of that event faded, and I found myself back in the grind of my daily existence as a single householder with children, the yearning for being remained. It was clear now something had truly shifted.

Shortly after returning from Burningman, John Troy arranged for a small troupe to visit Tiruvannamalai, India and Arunachala, its "sacred" mountain. Ramana Maharshi was devoted to the mountain, Arunachala, and always referred to it as Shiva, the formless Self. As you might expect, my expectations for this trip were high as I was expecting nothing short of a *Wizard of Oz* journey into a magical land resulting in the establishment in my total, permanent transformation.

Synchronicity enjoined us the entire journey. We arrived at our hotel with just enough time to freshen up before joining almost a million pilgrims in the full moon circumambulation of this sacred mountain. Oh my God! There were people growing out of the street with fifth stage symptoms of diseases we irradiated in this country thirty years ago. There were parentless dirty street urchins running around oxcarts and monkeys and sacred cows. Sannyasins were walking around in saffron robes blessing car fenders with potions.

135

On top of Arunachala, monks, surrounded by scores of monkeys, were igniting a giant cauldron of clarified butter or ghee into a sacred blaze for all to see. The feeling was of happiness and tranquility. I was awestruck. Here, a population of people I had pitied for their poverty was enjoying more genuine happiness than many Americans back home, besotted by their material goods.

The next day, we were taken by Ganesan into the bowels of the oldest temple in India, ceilings blackened with thick crusts of incense smoke accumulated over three millennia of rituals, and men in loin cloths tending fires in ancient subterranean caverns. Old friends were encountered in town; a beloved sage magically appeared on the back of a motorcycle at the last possible opportunity. Love songs were sung at the edge of a tranquil reflecting pond while a kingfisher delighted us with his plumage. Everything unfolded effortlessly; all in homage to the icon of the formless Self, Shiva.

I set off to on a trek up Arunachala to its peak, where the cauldron sat atop the sacred mountain. I had the gall to ask for more than I had already been given. I asked that a sign be given so that I would know for sure that I am being that which the mountain stood for. Two things then transpired. A stone from a cave that had sheltered the young Ramana Maharshi was picked up and given to me by our guide—a stone I had been quietly desiring but unwilling to take for myself. As we left the cave a large boulder of spiritual significance to the natives, "Shiva's Foot" was pointed out by our guide. As we neared the top a large bird could be seen soaring directly above this stone. I had never seen such a bird and was excited to learn from my guide that it was an eagle—only the second species of eagle I had ever seen. I turned to my companion, Paula, who was thirty yards below and shouted to her to look up at the eagle. At the moment we turned our attention to this eagle it stopped in mid-flight and beat its wings six or eight times—holding its position stationary in stillness during flight like a hummingbird. I was astonished. I did not think any other bird could accomplish this feat. This was yet another sign in a sea of synchronicity.

What's important to convey about this sojourn, however, is not that what happened was in itself so off the charts crazy wild cool that I had no choice but be blown away. No, it illustrates that the ordinary is transformed by the alchemy of Faith into the extraordinary. Not faith in a storyline, belief system or anything in particular. Faith in the Mystery that all is perfect and you are the theatre in which everything naturally occurs. When you are ready to re-cognize the non-physical reality that you are in freefall, the world of form confirms it for you everywhere.

Not long after our return from India, my friend, the Wizard, was invited to a return appearance on a local low-power radio station's program on spirituality called *Touchstone*. As it turned out, the show's host, Paul Nagy, was ready to let his role go, and I asked to take his place and the Wizard was happy to join me. For the next three years I would have the amazing grace of conversations with avant-garde sages from around the world in all walks of life. I was surprised that the established, largely unknown sages of our time would agree to have a conversation with me for free, a total spiritual newbie, on a micro-power FM station with a three-mile radius, albeit simulcast on the web, simply on the strength of an invitation by the Wizard. But there it was and I was not resisting!

Each week I would study the sages' books and pore over their Web sites, videos and blogs; anything I could get my hands on. I would celebrate their unique gifts, share their masterly elocution, probe them over any inconsistencies, and ask them for the spiritual solutions to my own dilemmas. Each and every time I was blown away by their nuanced grasp of this non-dual reality and their unique gifts for expressing it. One, Francis Lucille, had the grandfatherly sweetness of a fine wine mellowed with age. Another, Rupert Spira for example, possessed an unrivalled capacity to vivisect this dimensionless moment of now that would take you to and through the very door of presence. The younger sages such as Jeff Foster, Benjamin Smythe, Bentinho Massaro, Morgan Carraway, Lisa Cairns, Ilona and others, were fabulously in touch with the intimacy of "suchness" this "no-thing" this *Now*. Each one had a collection of pointer gems to share—the Truth processed through their unique experience. I began to have much greater respect for my ordinary fellow friends.

Gradually, over time, the circumspection offered by so many avant-garde sages that I had not known was supreme validation of the unbelievable reality that had been unveiled. I learned that an idea I had about Ramana Maharshi as a singular phenomenon taking place once in a millennia was far more commonplace than I could have imagined. Not only that, there were dozens if not hundreds of people in my local community so blessed. As a matter of fact, everyone I look upon is God in a different mask.

This is what it all boils down to. The whole spiritual exercise is simply meant to relax the mind and I-thought so that it will take a back seat to the headless heart of sentience, and allow life directly without the filters of judgment or veneer of words. When we live this way, or shall we say allow life to live us that way, ordinary life becomes extraordinary and divine. It's that simple.

I inevitably take the opportunity to acknowledge each and every one as the perfect divinity One already is. And every one totally gets it on some level. They may not have had the pretty words I have learned to express it, but each in their way is immediately ready to accept their inherent divinity. And why is that? All of us already intuit it at the deepest level. It is our condition at birth and it is still our condition underneath the garbage of all our learned ignorance. Coming into our spiritual fullness is not a finding of something new. It is the deconstruction and excavation job. Nothing brings me greater pleasure than to look through the bodily armour of another to witness the joyous Truth that we share together. It is the rush of God seeing God; Darshan. Nothing compares with this joy of sharing. Truly we are One. Let us share. Let us celebrate!

Yael Hana Powell

chapter 15

Yael Hana Powell

The Unhealed Life: Dancing with the Law of Love

I live in Paradise. Outside my window stretch pristine views of lake, rolling mountains and sky – a sky upon which every day is painted a sunset by the hands of Angels containing Messages of upliftment and beauty. Each morning when I awake, I find communion with the Nature Spirits all around me and with our Creator.

In meditation, I am lifted into a communion with Love that stretches me, dissolves me into the whole of God, fills me with the majesty and grace and mystery of the movement of Love that Creation is...taking my heart and making it a perfect expression of Love, granting me an experience of living Light, of the ever-moving hologram that God is, and giving me perspective, Love and guidance far beyond this human experience, beyond even the ability of the mind to comprehend.

Sometimes I am expanded into limitless Light, the luminosity alive with sizzling electricity, as if every electron is being switched on and I am pure life. There is only the tiniest thread to the awareness of "me," the "me" that is attempting to place words on the experience, that it might be shared.

Other times I am held in the Creator's Love, fully aware of myself as a stream of conscious Love, completely in bliss as my heart is acknowledged and all that I am shines into me, a gestalt of wonder, hyper-dimensional awareness, the ability to be the focal point of the heart of Love and the amazing, indescribable intricacy of relationships, of the aspects of Love that are alive within the Creator. Sometimes, especially when I have a specific prayer or need help with a situation in my human experience, this perspective is too vast.

Then I call on the beings of Love who assist us, and who, like us, create a bridge between this limitless Love and the experience we are having, day to day. The closest and most beautiful of these is my relationship with Jeshua (Jesus) who so lovingly focuses God's Love into the assistance that I need.

Whatever my experience, I am always aware of the pure unending Love that is ours to live and to share, to experience as our Creator and as the Creator's Love for us. I do my best to place into words these gifts of guidance and of unending Love. It leaves me breathless with awe, humbled by the mystery and filled with gratitude for the incredible gift of this communion with God that is ever ours, simply waiting to be accepted.

In my life I have true Love. My beautiful husband, Doug, Twin Flame, is a glorious heart with whom I share a completely different kind of communion, a communion of unconditional acceptance and a Love so deep it is eternal. Looking into his eyes, I experience home and once again, I am awed by the gift of my life.

I share my life as well with my soul sister, Shanna, whose Love for God is equal to mine, whose dedication allows my sometimes frustrating attempts at words on the mysteries of God to go out into the world to be shared. Every moment of my day I rejoice in the precious gift of my beloved animals. Every bark and purr are gems of Love in the shining necklace of this life.

I live in Heaven on Earth in every area but one: my every day is spent in pain. My body continually makes me aware of it.

Every step at times can be pure agony, every inch of my spine a blazing inferno. With every year that passes, my body becomes more distorted, something different from what I had envisioned. Yet, in those moments when I return from my cosmic traveling, shocked when the pain finds me again, I hear God whispering to me, "This is powerful. This is your gift, this unhealed life, it is a River of Love." At last, after forty years, I am able to listen and hear and to accept. In the past, it has not been so easy.

In 1983, I was given a diagnosis: a genetically predisposed disease for which there is no cure. Nothing can be done except to ameliorate the pain. I had been running from the reality already since age twenty. Finally it had a name – Ankylosing Spondylitis. I remember the day clearly. I was staying with friends in Little Rock, a long way from my home in Fayetteville. I stood in their living room alone. I put on Pachelbel's Canon in D and I proclaimed at the top of my lungs, "I am going to heal myself!"

I danced as best I could to the music and to my commitment to change this diagnosis. And oh, how I have danced this dance since then! I have danced with "You create your reality," step by frustrating step. I have danced it through the years in countless ways. I have done fasts for months at a time, consumed wheat grass juice that I ground myself, grew sprouts, ate raw, read books by the hundreds, changed diets, went to all kinds of healers, had many a "laying on of hands."

I have prayed. I have cried. I have yelled. I have stomped. I have done affirmations and visualizations. I have worked on myself until I could see my father, who had molested me from the crib, in perfect Love, as another being of God. I have worked with quantum healing. And I have walked the hallways of traditional medicine. I have been to pain clinics, seen pain management doctors. I even had

143

a pump placed in my abdomen in an attempt to have some respite from the constant pain. However, as soon as the pump was turned on and narcotics placed into my spinal cord, I very clearly received the Message from God, "If you do this, you will cut off your ability to receive these Messages from Me." And so I had the pump taken back out, another surgery.

All the while I have danced this dance, I had countless friends saying things to me such as, "What have you done to create this?" Every time, for so many years, I would become distraught. I would cry in despair and frustration. And yet, another reality kept coming in. I just wasn't able to listen.

In 1984 about a year after my diagnosis, a year that I had spent homeless and fighting for disability payments, the pain became so incessant and so completely overwhelming that, my life in shambles, unable to work, I decided I didn't want to live and began making plans to take my own life. I had been meditating at that point for twelve years and had received many gifts of guidance, intuitive flashes and experiences of powerful Love. I'd had amazing, clear communication with Nature, but my communion with Spirit had always been more nebulous, though I always felt the Light. As I made the decision to take my life and began collecting information, ordering books from the Hemlock Society, I also prayed for help. Help came.

It was a winter day. I had just gotten an apartment with government assistance, but even having a home couldn't alleviate the despair I felt. All the things I had loved to do—painting, hiking, my plans for a career—all were now impossible. I could barely feed myself. At that time there was no awareness of pain management. Doctors refused to give any meditation to people in chronic pain. The support group I had started for people in pain was filled with similar stories. Rather than bringing the upliftment I had hoped for, it too, increased the feelings of despair.

With a heavy heart, I sat to meditate. I could see the sunlight slanting through the little windows in my door. I sat in the one chair I could stand to be in, a lawn chair, a chaise lounge, yellow and white, and went into meditation.

The moment I did, I heard absolutely clearly, "Pick up your pen." I grabbed a notebook that I always kept beside me for writing poetry, and poised my pen over the paper. What began that day has completely changed my life, has given me my purpose and guided me step-by-step to this point, this place and this ability, at last, to fully listen.

What began that day was a communion with God so beautiful, so filled with Love, so clear, so tender, so personal, so intimate, and yet, so limitless that all I could do was do my best to use that pen and attempt to place words on the experience. At first all I could do was jot lines that were like poetry. Then, as I grew in confidence and practiced, I did better at capturing what was occurring.

At first, the Messages were filled with Love and support to get me through each day. Again and again I was told my life had greater purpose and that I had the strength to live it. Then, slowly, they began to expand to a vision of Love for humanity that was beautiful and profound.

Two years later, I met Doug. I had been waiting for him all of my life. I remember at five years old lying on the lawn looking up into the sky and feeling his presence and the absolute assurance that there was someone who was a part of my being. From that time throughout the years, I felt his presence regularly, more an energy that I recognized than any physical form, but so familiar to me, so clear, so specific that I knew I would recognize him anywhere.

In 1981 in meditation I was lifted into the realms of Light and given an experience of what I now would name Twin Flames. It was an experience of the mating of the forces of Creation, Light and life and power and joy and a unity of being that was shown to me as something that could be lived. I had no words to encompass the experience that was far beyond my rational mind. I did my best to hold on to the awareness. I even tried to explain it to the man I was with at that time. I finally gave up on the attempt.

Right before meeting Doug, the longing in my heart had reached a new level. I would sing at the top of my lungs with Peter Gabriel, "Bring me a higher Love." I sang it in the shower. I sang it in the car when I would take my little drives around the block just to get myself out of the apartment and stake my claim on some mobility.

Then, the week before I met him, I had a dream in which I saw his eyes. In the dream I was in a room I didn't recognize that was filled with people. Across the room there was a man who had his back to me and was looking out the window. Slowly he turned. His eyes met mine, eyes of the most amazing blue. In the dream we recognized each other. We left the building, got into a vehicle and asked each other who would steer and who would shift the gears. On waking I knew this was an important dream. What I didn't know was that it was about to manifest.

A week later, my best friend, Susan, insisted on taking me to a Sufi Camp that was happening about an hour away. For me, an hour's drive was nearly impossible but with the help of other friends, she made it work. She took my bed, put it in the back of a van and brought me to the place where I met my beloved. We've been together ever since. We spent the day with open hearts looking into each other's eyes. We couldn't speak because I was lying on the stage behind the teacher. Yet, something miraculous occurred and both of us recognized it.

I knew this was the one whom I'd been praying for. The first time that we sat together to meditate, the floodgates opened and suddenly, words of Love became available and I wrote and wrote, as fast as I could. Everything I had been shown about Love suddenly became clear and accessible. The reality of Twin Flame Love was undeniable; it was exactly what we felt. Together we were on fire, a flame burning in service to humankind. From that point on, as Doug and I made the choice to get married, we were guided impeccably every step of the way, and oh, how we needed that guidance!

In the beginning it was a relationship not only of the heart but of two strong egos with lots of baggage. I was in the midst of working through the issues around the incest with my father. Doug was a confirmed bachelor of thirty-five years. We would constantly "push each other's buttons." I would be overwhelmed with fear and he would want to run away, or run and hide and wait for me to find him.

At first, attempting to work everything out together, we worked with each other in counseling. The quicksand of the ego only grew more intense, until there were times when I thought it was impossible, that there was no way we would make it. I would go into meditation with tears streaming down my face and say, "God, please help! Please!" I would be lifted, lifted higher, up over the human perception and shown a vista of Love that was so beautiful that I knew that not only could we make it, we would. I was given steps, clear guidance that we could follow.

I was continually given a vision of Love that was so beautiful, so exalted, so filled with unconditional Love and acceptance and so filled with the living Spirit that it seemed almost impossible to comprehend. Even now we are amazed at what we were given then. Recently we went back and read the very first Message or meditation that I wrote when we came together and everything was there—things that it has taken us twenty-five years to truly live. Yet at the time all we could hear was, "Keep going." And we did.

So the first guidance that we clung to was that there is a Reality of Love that is "higher than" and so different from what we normally call Love that to choose it is to let go of all of our ideas of what we thought we needed and especially, of our desire to work things out on the level of the personality.

Next, I was shown the difference between the ego and the heart and reminded that every moment was a decision point. We were to ask ourselves continually which one we were choosing and to notice the truth about each—that the ego always creates separation, the heart always creates closeness. Over and over we were asked to choose the heart, to choose Love, to decide to be close. We would hold each other, in tears, both of us terrified of being hurt. But we chose Love and choice by choice, our relationship changed.

We came to recognize ever more clearly that the choice for the heart was possible and the choice for the ego always brought more distress. Guided step by step, we opened our hearts and at one point, we recommitted. I had just had surgery and Doug stood up for me. We remembered the power and truth of our Love, and from that choice, that deepened connection, almost instantly came Circle of Light, this place where we now live—a clear example of the heart's creation, of the Love of God shining, as we were told, through our hearts, to create our world.

In the beginning when Doug and I had only been together a few months, I ended up in the hospital, life-threatened, needing a transfusion, the result of a healing cure engaged in too passionately. In that hospital room was my first epiphany. As I sat to meditate, using the rolling table that goes over the hospital bed to write on, I was clearly shown that this body was a gift to the world ... that there was a reason that I had offered to wear it, to live in it, so that as I opened my heart, the resonance of Love combined with my experience could be a gift to the world—lifting up the suffering, loving the Earth free of her pain.

It was the first time that I heard the words "the unhealed life." Nonetheless, my resistance to the pain continued. No matter what I was shown in Spirit, the day to day reality of living in pain is so difficult, the pain so impossible to ignore. All the theories, all the information that I felt was true …that we create our reality, that we are purposeful creators…kept me continually engaged in working to change my experience.

So even while God whispered to me again and again, "This body is part of your service and it is purposeful as well as powerful," I truly could not accept it. I felt that it was my responsibility to bring the Light of God into the physical, especially since I knew with my whole being that it is possible and we are meant to do so. So, the dance continued.

In 1987, I received an extraordinary and life-changing Message. I had been sequestered by God, asked to refrain from reading any books, from receiving any spiritual commentary so that what I received could be clear and untainted by the experience or perceptions of other people. So I had heard nothing of those who

Chapter 15

were gathering. When I went into meditation, the Light was blazing as if the whole world were one glorious candle, fully lit and shining brightly. The chorus of the Angels, the vibrational "Hallelujah" made my heart ecstatic and bursting with joy. What I received, I called The LightWorkers' Decision.

I was shown that humanity had reached a turning point – that those who had come to serve humanity's awakening had come together in the realms of Spirit and made an offer... that we would transform not only what needed to be transformed for ourselves. We would transform by the Law of Resonance for all humanity. We would take on more than our share, that none be left behind. As I wrote, I sobbed. Tears streamed down my face, and I kept saying, "Yes, God, Yes! I make this commitment too." I was also shown clearly and powerfully the Law of Resonance – that whatever we have experienced in our lives, when we transform it into Love, then by the Law of Resonance, all who have had a similar experience are lifted up as well, and this was our commitment.

For the first time, I understood the power and the purpose of this unhealed life. I was also shown that I was here purposefully to transform a river of darkness, a river of incest and abuse that had been running through generations of a segment of humanity. Instantly I knew that this was true and my heart said, "Yes." With all my being I gave myself to God.

At the same moment that I was receiving the LightWorkers' Decision, others on planet Earth were celebrating the Harmonic Convergence, the exact day and the exact time, though I had never heard of it.

Yet, even now, the dance continued with, "You create your reality..." There were days when it seemed absolutely impossible that I could continue and I would cry in Doug's arms uncontrollably, telling him, "I can't do this." Always, he would simply love me and whisper, "Yes, you can and you will."

I was asked in meditation to use the word "God" for like so many others, I had found it uncomfortable, laden as it is with old baggage. I was shown that it is a word of power, the highest vibration word in the English language, and as with everything on Earth, we have to reclaim it for Love. So I began to call my meditations, my attempts at putting words on the ineffable, the Messages from God.

My communion with the Creator grew in ways hard to imagine in the mind's normal reality. When we moved to our piece of Heaven, Circle of Light, I would sit on the deck to meditate. I would be completely dissolved into the glorious whole of Love where everything is so beautiful and so majestically glorious, where the unfolding of ever new patterns of Light and the purpose of humanity as the Creator's heart would not just be shown to me—I was part of it.

The vibration was so exquisite, such ecstasy, that meditation became a different kind of experience and returning at that point, was agony. I would stand on the deck and cry at the return—not only because of the pain in my body but because of the return to a world that was rife with strife and killing and everyone hurting each other. Wars, poverty, all of it was unbearable after being in that Light.

Yet every time my heart would break over what I saw in the world, I would gently be shown a different view. It was a vision of the Reality of Love—that only Love is Real, that this experience of the world is a "sub-creation" of the mind. I would feel the truth then, clear and tangible: that right beside, or woven within, this world that we see with the "two eyes" of the ego-mind, there already exists the

151

Reality of the Heart, a bridge between this world and the pure realms of ecstatic Love. It is a world that is ours to choose.

In meditation this was illustrated for me in a very powerful way that has been of assistance ever since. I was sitting on my deck, my notebook in front of me, wrapped, filled, immersed in God's Love. Not only could I hear the birds singing; I could feel each and every one of them touching my heart, their song a very real vibration of Love. The breeze, the warmth of the sun, the expansiveness of the joy that I felt—all of it was an experience of a world of Love that truly could be named "Heaven."

I saw this reality; this experience I was having became like a picture on a computer screen and suddenly in front of it, there came another program that was the world normally experienced as the human drama. I could feel the tension in my solar plexus, the energy of worry and concern, the dull colors of limited perception and the over-all hypnotic trance that is the experience of much of humanity.

Then I was shown, very clearly, that both "programs" are running at the same time, just as on a computer. We have one program running in the background while another one is open before us. I was shown just how easy it is to click on the program running behind the one we see to bring it into the foreground so it takes up the whole screen and becomes the one that we are experiencing. Just so, with our reality, we can "change the screen" from the world of the ego to the world of the heart...from the world of duality to the world of only Love. All we have to do is make a choice. This Message, which I did my best to record, I named, "Change the Screen." It has been of assistance to me over the years since then and has also been helpful to many others.

As I said "yes" to the vision that God was giving me, the discrepancy between my experience in meditation and the world I return to began to diminish. I was also shown how the pulse of Creation comes through our hearts and goes forth in front of us to create the world we experience, and that our heart's beliefs—those things we had taken in and made a part of who we are—were what was showing up before us.

Slowly I began to be able to live it, to not only experience the beauty of God, the majesty, the wonder of all Creation, the astounding resonance of pure Love in meditation, but at last to be able to hold that resonance more and more through the days. Doug and I at that time were running another one of our old patterns. Like so many things, in meditation I would experience the glory of our Twin Flame unity, and then, face to face in the realm of the ego, we would dance the dance of withdrawal and longing, the button-pushing of the egoic consciousness. While it had changed so much, it hadn't changed enough.

One day I decided to "take the word of God and run with it." If what I was experiencing with Doug was the reflection of my own heart's beliefs, then it stood to reason that whatever it was, if I transformed it, my relationship with Doug would change. On the surface it seemed clear what was happening. Based on his experience as a child, Doug had a pattern of withdrawing. We understood it, and we named it. It was a very familiar companion.

Yet, according to what I had received, it was my own heart's reflection. So, I went to God in the shower, a place where I receive very clearly and said, "I want to be shown what this is. I want to see the heart's belief that is manifesting as this distance between me and Doug." I had to stomp my feet again and again. I had to proclaim at the top of my voice, "I want to see it!"

It takes some determination when we've hidden things from ourselves…

Suddenly, there it was. I saw what I had been holding and exactly how it was reflected. I lifted it into the Creator's Love and I felt the resonance change. Like a burst of Light, my heart felt free. That night Doug made a shift that has been our reality from that point on. It was a miracle. It was incredible. Suddenly the closeness, the unconditional Love, the acceptance—all the things I had longed for, at that point for fifteen years—suddenly became available. Our relationship shifted and the reality of the reflection of my heart was indisputable.

Gently, with such loving care and such indescribable expansion, God has guided me to this place of acknowledging the truth. I have to stand now to meditate because sitting is too painful, and my walking stick is a more regular companion, as I carefully negotiate being out of balance because my spine is so bent. Even while this body continues to manifest new conditions despite everything I've done...at last, I can hear what is being said, what I have been being shown now for twenty-five years. The Law of Love, the commitments of the heart supersede the ego's view of reality. What the ego rails against, the heart not only embraces but chooses.

Now, at long last I can read the words of Eckhart Tolle that are hanging on my wall, words that many times I've stood before in tears. Now they shine like a beacon on the truth of this life, "Accepting the unacceptable is the greatest source of grace in this world." In this acceptance the ego bends its knee and the mystery of life, the mystery of Love is revealed, the mystery that must insert itself into the mind's judgments of reality, allowing us to ask the deeper questions.

In our desire to name our reality, to get what we want, to name what we see, are we missing the greater messages of what Love truly is? How much can Love accomplish in and through us?

In meditation now, I continually experience what I have named "both/and." I am dissolved into the whole glorious unity of Love, exquisite, indivisible, ecstatic, and I am the individuation, a conscious stream of Love, an expression of a unique and precious nuance of the Love of God, in relationship with the Creator.

I am pierced by the sweet and indescribable gift of being loved and loving totally in return, even while I am part and parcel of the Love. Beyond time we are everything all at once. Through the opening of our hearts we are ready now for this communion—to live it and to let it live us.

Our lives here are both/and as well. We are the whole of humanity, the one heart and we are the individuated expression of conscious Love. In our own lives we are experiencing both as well.

How do we know which part of our lives can be changed as we shift our old beliefs, our old perceptions? And which parts of our lives are being lived in service to the transformation of humanity and this world? Here, too, I believe it is both/and. Guided every moment by the gift of our communion with God, we examine our heart's beliefs, lifting all of them into Love while at the same time knowing that everything we have lived, we have lived in service, and listening for our guidance about those things that are ours to accept unconditionally as our heart's greater reality.

We recognize also, even while we create the bridge world of Love, Heaven on Earth, that the reality of Love is far greater than anything we can imagine with our minds, and only our hearts can lead us there.

I can now embrace the following message received two years ago from Jeshua. It came in answer to my tearful prayers. At that point I couldn't accept the answer. Now I can.

"I am showing you your body from the perspective of the Divine, the levels of Love, from the quantum fields as they would be called today where everything is conscious and absolutely every iota of energy always has divine purpose. From this place of Light to Love, and Love to Love, and the extension of God to the hearts of humanity, I want you to recognize that every atom in your body, this body of God—not the body of a human being—every iota of the atomic energy of Love that makes up this matrix upon which your life is hung is a conscious being, and everyone is purposefully here in service to Love.

"Each one is holding the divine identity through resonance of a different aspect of the experiences of humanity's forgetting. Each one is committed to hold the reality of Love for that aspect of God that has been lost in the forgetting, until that resonance can serve its purpose in restoring the illusion, the reversal of Love back to the pristine and eternal truth of what Love is as the true identity of every person. It holds this not only as this atom of your heart but as the energy field of your real countenance until you can allow yourself to then be expressed as the 'en-conscious-ment' of Heaven meeting Earth, of the place where the deepest reversal of Love can turn and remember its truth, atom by atom."

This body contains every resonance of the whole experience of humanity around the belief in pain and suffering. It is not my belief. It is my service. Allowing my Love to embrace this imperfect vehicle, I realized recently, as my heart soared in joy even while my steps were so difficult, that now at last, I am able to live the truth: that this isn't suffering at all. It's only Love.

I can feel it now deep within me. What I've been shown through all these years has now become me—that the reality of Love is always giving. It truly is in giving that we receive. Now I hold in my heart the whole of humankind and open as completely as I possibly can to that magnificent flow of Love, that as it flows through me, I become transparent. It plays the song of Love on this instrument that is my body, tunes up every cell, every wave length of pain, every experience I have had in this incarnation, attuning it as it flows onward in giving to perfect Love as the heart of humanity.

As Jeshua further said, "The One then becomes revealed in the perfect point of the dance where the identities of the world meet the place where Love is received as the Real identity, as the heart of God. That place, that meeting place is so powerful. It is the point, the place, the energy field where the transformation of the world is accomplished.

"Everything that is happening now, all the changes and all of the drama are only to lead people to the place of willingness for hearts to open and the true identity of Love to be revealed, to restore the truth to every story and bring about the story of the son/daughter of God resurrected, restored, returned to only Love that the pocket of reversal may at last be healed and the purpose of Love revealed as already accomplished."

Now, I truly can feel everyone, all of us, this one heart together as God continually shows me that we are "both/and." We are both the magnificent unity that is the whole of Love and we have the astounding gift that is the gift of our relationship with our Creator. As we receive this resonance of truth and beauty, accept it and allow it to rush onward to be a blessing, to be the attunement of humanity, we become Love incarnate, the heart of the Creator acknowledged in joy.

* * *

Yael Hana Powell published her first article entitled *The Unhealed Life* in 1989 in *The Sun*. She is the author of seven books. Yael describes herself as a mystic, her communion with God the center of her life. Yael lives in the beautiful Ozark Mountains in Eureka Springs, Arkansas with her husband, Doug, her soul sister, Shanna, two Pomeranians and five cats, four fish and myriad of Nature Spirits. More about Yael and her work, including the most recent Messages from God can be found at www.circleoflight.net

chapter 16

Kimberly Rex, MS©

Making Yourself at Home

The qualities of feeling at home in not so much a place as it is an experience. Making yourself at home is acknowledging the feeling of safety, nurture and trust within yourself. It can be experienced as quantum, cellular, body-mind-spirit, and developmentally related to community, country, hemisphere, planet, galaxy and universe. At this moment, you are experiencing all aspects of home. The questions are: *"Do you feel at home?"* and *"What is your quality of life in the present?"*

Your inner dialogue, sense of space and time, as well as the meaning you give your experience impacts how you perceive life and making yourself at home in any given moment

<u>In Your Own Body</u>

You spend 100% of your time here. There are an estimated 50 trillion cells, 600 muscles, and hundreds of thousands of neurotransmitters, as well as twelve energy meridians and a chakra system that make that inform your inner home. The muscles, tissues, organs, glands, enzymes, hormones, amino acids, etc. are all in communication. It is like the United Nations on a microbiological level. This information and communication between these systems help you navigate life on a daily basis. When one part of the system is out of sync or balance, this affects the quality of energy communication between the systems of your body.

The cells of your body have a binary response. They move towards growth and communicate with other cellular systems when there is safety, nurture and calm. They shut down when there is significant stress, blockage or interruption of energy flow.

Taking care of your health empowers this communication. Getting nurture from whole foods, clean water, spending time in nature, and full-spectrum light nourishes your body: home. You are designed for success and self-healing. When you resonate with these life enhancing actions, you move into stewardship of the vehicle that allows you to experience life. As you resonate with valuing life itself, your vision of receiving support and nurture from Earth takes on the meaning of relationship. It is through this connection that you have the opportunity to see the impact your actions have on the planet you live on: home.

In Your Own Mind

Feeling at home within your own body is directly related to your sense of feeling energized and nurtured. It depends greatly on your ability to feel supported and receive benefit from that support. The ability to give and take what is beneficial to you, and to let go of what is not useful helps to discern what will nourish your body-mind system.

Everything in the Universe is communicating in vibration, wave and particle creating a response or form. This includes your emotions, thoughts, arguments, as well as your joys and successes. You are taking part in the symphony of the Universe! The frequency signatures of your emotions serve a purpose. They give you feedback about to where you are in the present. Your body is a map of your life's experiences.

Awareness of feelings and response originate early in your development as a human being. Relationships and interactions with others are based on needs. You have both life and spirit level needs that start at conception. They impact how your experience life, connection and nurture.

Feelings in the present may be directly related to what has happened to you over time. Unconscious material of earlier experiences and automatic responses from your Autonomic Nervous System manage your response to life. Your emotional, thinking and survival brain contribute to how you experience life in the present.

Everything in the Universe is communicating in vibration both in wave and particle form. This includes your emotions, thoughts, arguments, as well as your joys and successes. The frequency signatures of your emotions serve a purpose. They give you feedback about where you are currently. Your body is a map of your life's experiences.

Dr. Ray Castellino and Dr. William Emerson suggest that everything that happens to you prenatally, during your birth process, and your first years determine how you respond to life's challenges. It is the blueprint for your relationships. Being seen and heard for who you are, and allowed to explore and return to the safety of your caretakers impacts how you perceive life and relationship.

If life needs are not met in coherent ways early on, your ability to resonate with understanding, appreciation, forgiveness and love for self and others diminishes. You can only see and experience the wholeness of another to the degree you can see and feel the wholeness of yourself. Healing internal conflict brings peace to your body-mind system, and expands your capacity for loving relationships.

According to Bert Hellinger, the founder of *Family Constellations,* there is an order between generations, partners, siblings and extended family. The order of love enhances the ability to take vital energy and wisdom from your family.

Inner conflict transforms to greater inner peace through the ability to include your ancestors and bring greater harmony, health and balance to your life through facing life and doing something good with this information. Hellinger's work also validates the interaction between family members and other groups through war, intolerance, abuse and differences affect our current experience of inner peace and health. This can be healed in the present by looking at the patterns, unresolved conflict and feelings in your own life.

Noticing how you feel and then responding to that feeling gives you insight into what you resonate with in the moment (where your life energy is dedicated). Having the opportunity to choose your response is a gift of freedom.

"Between stimulus and response there is a space. In that space is our power to choose our response. In our response lie our growth and our freedom." ~ Viktor E. Frankl

Viktor Frankl developed the *Logotherapy* after having been incarcerated in the Concentration Camps of the Holocaust. He brought love to his own experience and to others while he endured the harshness, loss and severity of the situation. He chose to experience positive regard for every person including the prison guards. His choice to love over hate helped him to survive the horrible conditions. He went on to share what he learned in this more than challenging situation with others that he shared with the world through his work.

You see with your mind through the filters of memory. This has a direct effect on your breath, posture, range of vision and attitude.

Frankl called upon the love he experienced with his wife and family, and recalled the importance of love and life purpose when he chose to stay connected to this basic human life need.

Knowing that you have a choice to empower your memory allows you to update your experience whenever you wish to expand and access more light, life energy and expansive vision of what is possible. You are designed for success and self-healing.

<u>In Your Heart</u>

Your heart is the place where you gain wisdom. By placing loving regard, appreciation or a feeling of joy consciously in your heart area, you are able to affect the function of your entire body-mind system. To do so, become aware of your breath and focus in your heart before speaking. This expands the electromagnetic fields of the heart and brain for better clarity, problem-solving, connection to love, courage, compassion and intuition. It helps you to respond to challenges or problems informed by your heart and mind instead of fight or flight reaction.

Clarity, truth, and expression of your own needs with respectful wording creates greater presence. Experiment with this idea by reading the paired sentences below noting how you feel as you read both.

<u>Indecision to Clarity</u>

"Maybe, I'll call you to tomorrow." / "I'll call you tomorrow."

"Yeah, I think that song is great." / "Yes, that song is great."

"Nah, I don't think it's a wise decision." / "No, it's not a wise decision"

<u>Diminishing to Valued</u>

"I'm just a student." / "I am a student."

"I can't exercise for thirty minutes." / "I choose not to exercise for thirty minutes." or "I am not willing to exercise for thirty minutes."

The first step is awareness. As a practice, start by listening more deeply to how you speak to yourself and others. Carry a pocket-sized journal to record some of messages about your goals, your opinions and your decisions. Choose a few word changes to enhance clarity, vitality and choice. Observe how your energy level and commitment change with these new messages.

Getting in touch with basic life needs helps you understand what you are experiencing.

<u>Basic Life Needs</u>

Bonding-Closeness-Harmony-Nurturing-Security-Trust-Sleep-Protection-Boundaries-Positive Touch- Appreciation-Respect-Being Understood-Space-Light-Play-Laughter

Carry this list with you as you go through the day. Feelings are messengers for you that will make a difference in the quality of your wellness and sense of well-being. When you are feeling some form of stress or come to a standstill in a conflict producing feelings of anger, shame, guilt or fear, look at your list. Is there something on this list that stands out for you? What need is speaking most?

Example: You are feeling overwhelmed by deadlines, and don't not enough downtime. You feel angry because it feels as if there is no end to the amount you have to do, and the list continues to get bigger.

When you find yourself blaming your boss, your partner, and family, check your Basic Life Needs List. Do you need SPACE, SLEEP or RESPECT? Is there something you need to express? Do you need to set loving boundaries? Is there a new awareness about a need that you haven't seen before? How does this awareness make you feel?

A communication from the perspective of compassion might be: "I feel sad and tired when I work long hours to get the boss his reports because my need for sleep and time with my family are not being met when I work after hours without taking a break." Notice that the focus is on your needs.

Marshall Rosenberg, author of *Non-Violent Communication*, states that focusing on needs is also helpful in communicating with others. When communicating with your boss you might say, *"My need to spend a few hours with my family in the evening... is making it a late night for me to complete these reports accurately and my needs are not being met."*

165

"Could we talk about some options that would help to complete the reports during work hours?"

Notice that the communication is based on possibility and respect. Finding ways to be inclusive is compassionate. It is well worth the time and energy to explore this communication style. It will help you feel more at peace in yourself, in your relationships and enhance your experience of compassion on the planet!

Love helps orient you to what is life-energizing and healing. This is true for the cells of your body, between family members, partners, as well as communication between nations. Life is an interconnecting web of connection based on needs. It is important to acknowledge that we each have needs for connection and harmony in our lives. The process of identifying and healing these needs starts at the personal level.

"Everything we do is in service of our needs. When this one concept is applied to our view of others, we'll see that we have no real enemies, that what others do to us is the best possible thing they know to do to get their needs met." ~ Marshall Rosenberg

When there is coherent flow of energy between people in a relationship, there is both motivation and capacity to build on differences, expression of loving and healthy boundaries and a drive to return to union or stability. How you observed your parents moving through conflict creates an imprint of what conflict means to you, and how and if conflict can be resolved. Your conflict style may, in fact, be a response or reaction to what you observed in your early experience of life.

Non-coherent energy flow in a relationship leads to the feeling of inadequacy, of blaming others for your feelings and pain. It can also result from an inability to accept the other for who and where they are. Arguments, negative habits, and behaviors deplete each person in the relationship. This can result in anger, depression, guilt or shame. These feelings are messengers that help you listen to what needs your attention in your life, and what unmet need is not being heard or met.

A loving relationship is not about being free of stress or resistance. It is about reaching greater compassionate understanding of self and other. Places where your personal life needs have not been resolved are opportunities for gaining awareness and healing. This means looking at non-coherent patterns, issues of resistance, and the type of relationship issues you attract. Resolving them internally creates new patterns and possibilities for greater harmony.

"The fruit of self-understanding is self-acceptance. The fruit of self-acceptance is self-love. The fruit of self-love is love for the world. The fruit of love for the world is service to the world. The fruit of service to the world is peace." ~ Russell Rowe

Empathy is an expression of love. When you can connect and truly listen to another there is greater capacity for contentment, peace of mind and understanding. It empowers you and others to reach for the *win:win* in terms of needs. When you appreciate what you have learned from your challenges, it helps you integrate new awareness into your life so you can grow from the experience.

Empathy leads to greater sense of calmness, understanding and bonding. It also helps you meet challenging situations in your life with greater life energy, support, enthusiasm and joy. When you understand that every human being has the same basic life needs, you have greater respect for humanity as a whole.

In Your Spirit

Chapter 16

Your spirit is the core essence of yourself. You are both taking part in the symphony of frequencies that are creating the fabric of the Universe, and the Universe itself. The quantum world is a fractal for the Universe at large. There is more space than matter, and everything is connected. Unified and String Theory suggest that there is a web of connection between everything. Changing your perception or resonance with events, relationships and experience, changes how you meet life. When you change how you see the world, the world you experience changes.

On the Planet

From space, Earth can be seen as a blue planet. The oceans connect continents and nourish life in every form. The water you drink has been part of a legacy of information from the first forms of life on this planet. The water you drink today is the water that the dinosaurs, Mozart, and Michelangelo once shared. In this way, you are partaking in the process of sharing a home with the past, the present and the future. Your body-mind system relies on the elements of the Earth. According to the Chakra System from India, life is only possible due to the elements of the Earth, Water, the sun or Fire, and Air directly, and these are translated into energy for your benefit through your body-mind system. They are spinning energy reservoirs that maintain physical, emotional and mental functioning in the human body.

The Earth Chakra located at the base of the spine enables you to receive frequency patterns from the earth as well as its food.

The Water Chakra (pelvis) allows for electrical communication throughout the body. Every cell is filled and surrounded by a fluid environment. Like the Earth, we are 70% water. The Fire Chakra (solar plexus) helps you to receive warmth.

Without the sun, life would not be able to continue. The Air Chakra (heart) allows you to assimilate air or breath. Oxygen carries the energy that creates and sustains life.

These basic needs are not only for our physical body, but have correlations with our emotions and attitudes about life. The throat chakra is the space out of which emotions and yearning for the Divine emerges. The Brow Chakra is related to thinking function, and is associated with the pineal gland. It is said in meditation traditions that the Brow and Crown Chakra are the place of mind and soul entwining.

In the Universe

You are a multidimensional being of sound and light. Life is energy in motion. E-motion changes the landscape of your home and affects the direction of your inner compass heading on the map you travel in life. Expanding your conscious awareness expands your ability to experience your connection to Universal wisdom.

The Universe is broadcasting information every second. What you resonate with receiving will match what you receive. Literally, like a radio station, you tune in to the frequency patterns that are currently playing in your body-mind system. As you begin to cleanse the filters of your perception, you become more aware of synchronicity and support from the Universe itself. New possibilities become more frequent. This helps to inform and support your life and spirit purpose.

Current science confirms that every bit of matter in the Universe can be traced to its origin. The expression of light and matter through space and time translated itself into gases, materials, stars, planets, and life forms. You are literally a being of light experiencing life because of these beginnings. You are carrying all time and all space within you! Because of this, every moment is an opportunity to experience the expansive and creative adventure of life. Your map is the cosmos and frequency is your song. You are part of its music, its light and its evolution. Make yourself at home!

* * *

Kimberly Rex, MS© is a Certified Resonance Repatterning Practitioner and can be found at www.windowstotheheart.net

Tony Samara

chapter 17

Tony Samara

Joyous Communication

How can I honestly express myself when I fear that others will think less of me? How can I be true to my heart when I fear the reactions of the person that I would like to be able to be truthful to?

During the various seasons as we are meeting with many people familiar and unfamiliar this is a perfect time to be conscious of a new way of dealing with old situations that no longer serve a purpose.

There is no purpose in creating fear or anger within yourself or in others. There is no purpose in bringing your heart to a space where joy and light fade into the mundane disappointments and disillusionments that are inevitable when we go down a well-trodden path that leads to nowhere.

There is a purpose though to practice what it means to be free and conscious. The purpose being that we give less of who we are to the old and move forward to a space that is uniquely in this moment by focusing on the joy and freedom of what it means to be conscious. Conscious of the parts of yourself that make you uniquely human and more. Conscious of the parts of you that celebrate this moment in a completely free way.

We need to be clear that the burden of the old no longer needs to be our paradigm but rather the birth of the new light that is forever inside of our hearts. This will make everyone joyous and change the structure of the situation that is causing the sense of confrontation.

In a practical sense, once this thought is brought into the light of your consciousness there are a few steps that are easy to practice to make this a reality in all the different situations. The situations that as human beings we find ourselves in and are challenged to make visible our unique truth in each moment.

Some people do not like confrontation. Some people do not like it when people confront them or when there is a situation which requires a confrontation as the best way to proceed. Some people prefer to run away from the issues requiring confrontation.

Instead of looking at confrontation as an issue that will cause pain and thus continue to practice the method of avoiding the issue, why not utilize your heartfelt communication in a new way.

Take a deep breath. Relax all the muscles in the body and focus on the love and consciousness that comes from the space of being in this moment. Choose this harmonious consciousness rather than getting caught up in the idea of pain. The pain is simply based on belief systems from the past and ideas of possible painful futures rather than the unique presence of this actual moment.

Joyous Communication is the Way

With every aspect of your communication, rather than bring in the pain of the past or the fear of the future, express the joy of what it means to be able to move through this wonderful lesson to a space that brings you closer to the joy of being in deep communication with another wonderful human being.

Instead of pretending nothing is wrong or escaping into your old pattern and belief systems, which often blows things out of proportion as your pain is projected onto the pain that you feel this communication is causing, there are some easy steps you can take to transcend rather than try to resolve the issue.

The first step is to completely come into your center and not to utter any words until you have taken a few deep breaths and calmed your body into a normal, relaxed state. Take a few moments to analyze what it is that your body is actually feeling in this moment. Especially the shoulders, the jaws, the thighs, the mouth. If they are not relaxed, take a few more moments to consciously feel that these parts of your body are flowing with the warm sensation of love.

The next step is to observe what the communication is really about. Most of us get caught up in the feelings that are triggered by a communication and hence communicate from the feelings that are triggered rather than the actual communication that may help transcend the block. This is called projection and hence what we are asking the people we are communicating with is for them to react to our projection. Then we can continue a vicious circle of understanding our pain rather than finding freedom and consciousness in the situation that truly requires this.

When you continue the process of joyous communication you are more easily able to evaluate clearly what is going on, what is happening, and hence comprehend what is actually affecting the behaviors and conditions creating the situation that is not bringing you joy.

It is important to differentiate the pain from the past or from the future or from the expectations of the future and remain an observer. This means dropping criticism, judgment, subtle provocations and sarcasms, blaming, causing pain or whatever mechanisms whereby you, the observer, becomes the pain.

When you are in this free space of observation notice how you feel. Notice the feeling that is free from projection and is simply discerning the situation from a conscious space. Discernment does not come from feeling but rather from compassion and love that are embracing and expansive no matter what the situation is.

From this space we can create thinking that becomes more intelligent and is more able to express our deeper communications which always contain love, compassion, joy and kindness.

Connect with this depth of consciousness in your communication and trust. Deeply understand that all your needs will be met from this space in relation to what is happening and how you are feeling.

Express what you want from this depth rather than what you don't want. Affirm in a positive way that what you want is a reality that you trust and know to be possible rather than affirming the blocks and projections in yourself or in other people that confrontational communication thrives on.

Make sure that your affirmations are not demands either crude or subtle. Make sure that you do not create a sense of guilt, fear, shame, insecurity but rather that your affirmations create a space of open embracement that allow for yourself and others to feel the joy of this communication.

Make sure that your communication gives rather than takes. Giving only comes from a space of abundance and consciousness. Part of giving is being able to listen. Giving yourself the gift of listening is giving yourself opportunities that only come when we are able to hear the wisdom not only in ourselves but in all that is around helping us to grow into this sense of oneness and joy.

What a wonderful reality to affirm in all our communications so that every aspect of life becomes more real, more human and more full of compassion for ourselves and all living beings.

Conscious Relationships

From the moment we are born, the most important aspect of life becomes relationship. Relationship is central for survival and for a sense of belonging and well-being. To understand relationship is to understand that this is what makes us human.

In the beginning we learn to relate to what is closest and most dear to our hearts and this is the love that a mother has for her child. We understand that relationship is an expression of love, a sharing of love and a communication of love.

Most of us forget this core aspect of relationship, as unfortunately our mothers are human and even though deep inside there is love the mundane and practical expression of this gets distorted and the child begins to need love rather than express love.

This sense of neediness is what our society has condoned as normal and acceptable. Hence it is difficult to see this neediness as it is such a core aspect of how we see the world.

A child gets frustrated when the mother needs time to focus on other things than the relationship to the child. This creates even more need and so the relationship becomes distorted and as the child grows older this distortion carries on to the relationship he/she has with friends and ultimately with the relationship he/she has with their partner.

I see the world today as suffering from a lack of conscious relationship and full of what I term "needy" relationship. I see this

Tony Samara

as the cause of many worldwide problems that aren't always attributed directly to this issue.

Over the next months I will be working with conscious relationship in order to help this to be easily put into practice. Let us embrace conscious relationship in all its aspects so that we can release this neediness and allow our lives to become filled with love.

Conscious Nutrition

A wonderful way to support and encourage greater balance and peace in your life is to be more aware of the subtle, yet profound ways that food is affecting us and the world every day, on a physical, mental and emotional level.

For example, eating heavy, dense food can leave us feeling heavy and dense.

Eating more light and vibrant foods encourage us to feel light and more vibrant!

We make life much easier for ourselves on all levels when we give our body optimum foods that require a minimum of effort to digest whilst giving maximum possible nutrition and life-force.

The subject of nutrition is not simply a question of the food we eat at meals.

Besides nutrients, foods contain scents, colors and invisible particles that attract pure light, light that is so essential for our joyful life and well-being.

The choices we make are thus of great significance.

The difference between flesh-based and vegetarian foods lies in the amount of sunlight they contain.

177

Fruits and vegetables are so steeped in sunlight, that one could say they are a condensed form of light.

In order to develop the qualities of the heart, besides eating peacefully, consider eating consciously.

This means bringing in more light by eating foods full of concentrated light.

These foods contain the beautiful sounds that connect our hearts to the rhythms and invisible aspects of the Universe.

Your future depends on how you eat and what you eat.

Focusing on organic fresh fruits and vegetables that are in season is a way to connect to Nature and its rhythms and cycles so that one may be in harmony with it.

Nature is an omnipresent guide and a reference to how human beings can live harmoniously on the planet.

Optimum Foods

All fresh, ripe fruit and vegetables (raw and local is ideal)

Sprouted seeds, grains and beans (e.g. sunflower seeds, quinoa, mung beans)

Sea Vegetables (e.g. spirulina, dulse, wakame, nori)

Superfoods (e.g. hemp seeds, goji berries, wheatgrass)

Cultured Foods (e.g. sauerkraut, tempeh, kefir)

Such a diet would exclude foods that deplete the body of light such as meat, fish, poultry, eggs and refined foods such as white sugar, white flour, deep frozen and/or processed foods.

Food manufacture is one of the most water intensive activities in the world and it takes far less water to produce plants than meat. A vegetarian diet helps to decrease water consumption and pollution.

The vast amount of land used to raise animals is causing environmental problems such as habitat destruction and deforestation. Going vegetarian will halve the land-use of your diet.

Your body is your temple and every action within the temple, done with conscious intention, creates a more harmonious outcome.

The secret to opening the treasure-house of food, is the love and compassion attained within your consciousness.

The treasure is the sun, condensed into particles, which we can send to all the centers in our bodies.

By choosing your foods consciously you break the cycle of action and reaction.

You become light in the world - dissolving unconsciousness in the light of your new way of eating.

You become a reflection of consciousness in a most pure form.

Frequencies that are Now Embracing the Earth

I feel more than ever that humanity has the possibility to realize the potential state of Wholeness, or Completeness, that is incrementally achieved by those who choose to heighten their thoughts or whose mind, words and deeds are authentically harmonious and serene so as to be in touch with deep wisdom.

It is surely the goal of physical existence to achieve this full state of wholeness and it can be partially experienced during ones progress to its full achievement.

It is a state where ignorance and superstition are superseded by an awareness of frequencies that speak beyond such limitations to the innate intelligence that is present beyond the lower man made frequencies that have kept humanity in the dark for so long.

I believe that this expansion of light is now perceived on many levels around the world and has a real consequence that becomes clearer day by day!

There is no dualism of good or bad or even that today is better than yesterday but rather a growing awareness that brings us closer to what it really means to be human in this very moment!

I believe that there is no evil in nature. Hurricanes, earthquakes, volcanoes and sicknesses, which humans believe to be nature's wrath or a manifestation of lower forms of vibration or punishment for man's misdeeds, are for me ethically neutral. That is they are neither good, nor bad in themselves. They are either the products of chance, the existence of which is necessary to allow freedom of choice, or they are a function of an aspect of the universal laws of nature, necessary to uphold creation.

For me all is totally good in essence, thus all creation is good and is functioning as it was designed to and, as our mind expands beyond dualistic and judgmental thoughts, we slowly come closer to this natural wisdom inherent in the universe.

Negativity is the product of humanities wrongful choices and it is easily eliminated by choices that bypass such inherited fallacies that limit our higher perceptions. Today it may seem that these fallacies and negative human traits abound only because as we all let go of what has limited humanity for so long, we let go of so many of these collective destructive aspects that the Hindus refer to as the Kali or that I refer to as ignorance.

On the surface it may seem to many scientists, environmentalists, economists and artists around the globe that indeed we are in an era where what we know is being destroyed by the turbulence that we are facing. I would say it is more like the Phoenix is rising from the ashes of such destructive forces and their obsolete paradigms.

I would strongly emphasize that the Phoenix within or the birth of awareness can be acquired and refined within each one of us no matter what the circumstances we face may be. It comes more easily to those who choose to reflect and meditate with a bright, clear and unbiased mind and hold close to heart the real core values of life.

The aware mind is capable of logical and precise thinking with clarity of thought that is free from preconceptions, and is thereby able to perceive this higher frequency that resonates in all aspects of life rather than being a far removed philosophical or esoteric concept. However, it is important to note that logic and rationality of thought are not the only requisites of what it means to be human in a more complete sense.

A wise human being has a mind that tempers rationality with benevolence. It is the mind that having perceived the innate goodness of life becomes benevolent and more light; thinks for and of the highest and most noble aspects of life and is committed to it.

As this essence indwells in human beings, it can easily be acquired by a clear choice to think, speak and act in accordance with the higher frequencies inherent in such actions. So in actuality it is one of the principal means for achieving the goal, and at the same time part and parcel of that same goal.

This goal, the Lighter existence, made more accessible by such frequencies as are present today, becomes more powerful as our focus moves towards the light rather than remain in the shadows of the mind. I have no doubt that humanity's natural inclination is moving towards such higher frequencies that may well only become more clear with hindsight.

As the Phoenix flies higher towards the realms of light we will have the clarity it takes to be creative in a more conscious and wise way with our hearts wise enough to feel the new freedom that helps create a life-affirming paradigm!

Letting Go of Old Structures

In the world today people are saying to themselves, that we have had enough of the old paradigms and the old systems and we want to change. We don't know what we want to change, we don't know how to change but we want to change and that clarity creates a power that has a very real and powerful effect in the world. It changes what most people thought a few years ago was quite impossible to change and that is not even through conscious spiritual work, that is just through the intention being so strong that it changes and pushes away the old paradigms so that there is the possibility and the space that allows the birth of something new.

There are spaces that are opening and in the beginning they seem to be very distant and we cannot connect to them, but as we become more conscious and more clear and put our heartfelt spiritual work into practice then it is possible to utilize our intention to bring forth those changes in a much more conscious way. Then we are walking the path to a depth of our heart and this means that we will be supported.

I believe that we can as human beings assist this movement by being conscious and this is why I would like to share with you a very interesting meditation, which if we put it into practice today and in the future and especially in the next few weeks/months, where there will be more changes, more difficult changes that we will face as a collective group of human beings here on this beautiful earth, then we can move towards the birth of something new rather than get stuck in the fear that the old is there and that we can't actually deal with it.

We can let go of those old structures and trust that as we jump into the space that is unknown to the mind and the space that is unknown to the innermost part of yourself, that behind all those things there is the heart, and the heart will support you to a beautiful harmony which is present in this moment, but that you can through this meditation bring into more presence not just for yourself but also for the many people who are perhaps dealing with situations that are more difficult than yours, that would feel very happy to receive this beautiful meditation through your intention, through your practice; happy to receive the space that it creates—that is a birth of something that is new no matter what the situation is, however difficult, whatever it is, there is always a beautiful learning that happens and the beautiful transformation that happens that then gives that situation real meaning.

So no matter what is happening in Japan or the Middle East, there is a depth of meaning in that situation that feeds the heart of those individuals that are dealing with this situation and we can help that by connecting from our own heart space through this meditation, through expanding our consciousness so that we are clear where our intention is put so that we join in that transformation that is not just individual to yourself, but that becomes a world transformation that helps us to move beyond the pain and the suffering, back to the space that the heart loves and that is love itself.

Meditation is a Natural State of Being

Everybody can meditate as it is a natural state of being—like sleep, like relaxation--everyone has it in them to experience this.

The major obstacle is that our focus has been removed from certain aspects of ourselves in order to deal with a more core survival issue, which is essential in a very complex world, such as it is in the western world. It is not that the complex world is a bad thing it simply means that our attention forgets how to relax at times, how to meditate, as our mind and emotions get full of so many other things.

So the goal of meditation in the beginning would be to unlearn that which prevents the natural state of being from being a real experience.

Meditation is not like some people may think sitting down and stilling the mind - it is a state of consciousness and awareness that allows for creativity and action but in a different way than rushing around from one place to another.

It has been shown through various researchers at universities that meditation actually helps one to improve creative abilities, emotional intelligence and even improves IQ. The reason for this is that meditation allows the natural flow to all other aspects of yourself to be much more in tune with what makes you alive. It is just like when you sleep, you wake up refreshed and clear. It is just like when you relax, you are able to let go of the stresses that seem so intense in that moment. Meditation helps the flow of life energy so that you feel a joy and a clarity that is part of the creative process of meditation.

This is never achieved simply by sitting down, it is a much more complex process. Our idea of meditation being sitting quietly in a corner for twenty minutes is quite misleading.

How to Be Free from Fear

For me, fear is a major problem in western and eastern societies, and today even in most native societies, because we get dictated to so much by lacks and limitations based on fear. For example, the fear of not having enough or the fear of being alone or the fear of not being accepted or the fear of not being good enough or the fear of not living to your expectations or someone else's expectations. It can go on forever; there are thousands and thousands of fears. They take up a lot of energy—a lot of physical energy beyond what we realize, a lot of emotional energy and a lot of mental time. They dictate a lot of our actions and to be fearless is an amazing sense of freedom. It's a freedom where it doesn't mean you're perfect but you can make choices that are not dictated by "I have to do this because if I don't do this then this and this and this will happen."

I find that children are fearless. Children are more creative, more open and more able to adapt to situations very quickly and enjoy those changes much more than some people.

I was reading that because of the economic crisis many people are committing suicide because their reality is changing so much and the fear becomes so immense. They don't know how to cope with it so they just say "This is too much for me," and they can't see that perhaps the situation is a gateway to an immense change and the realization of something that couldn't happen without that change.

So for me, being fearless is being open and creative and joyful.

When you are able to be free in that sense, you open your mind to a creative knowledge and wisdom that goes beyond what we can see. I find that some people in such situations think of things that they never thought of that actually just come forth and help them in a way that is so powerful.

I've known people who have lost their jobs and it's been a crisis for sure, and painful, and not nice, but they have told me they would have never changed that experience because what it has shown them is to do something totally different. To maybe reassess their values and reassess their priorities in a way that allows them to do something that they wouldn't have done before because things were going in a way that was okay. Losing the job has pushed them to the edge and I think that's what letting go of fear is. It's going to the limits of what you feel comfortable with so that you can really look at what is out there and be open to all of those things, all of the possibilities out there.

But what can you do? You know that you're fearful, that you're afraid, that you're panicked. What is the next step?

One step is not to get so serious. Many people, when a crisis hits and their fear overwhelms them, tend to spend a lot of time trying to resolve the problem using their mind or using the old programs in the mind to try to resolve whatever. They spend time thinking, talking to friends in a way that, really it's useful for a little while but doesn't actually address the problem. So for me, the first step is to move beyond the fear by raising the energy inside of your body.

One way to move that is, moving the body. Rather than sitting down, I would take up an interesting exercise like walking or dancing and just do something. Move, because the movement actually moves things inside of your mind, and breathe - breathe deeply into your belly so that you can see that perhaps there is more than just that old program that is coming up.

Next, it is good to be open and watch the signs around you—watch interesting synchronicities, interesting things that tell you perhaps to move in a direction that seems totally crazy. Your friends may say, "Are you sure you can do this?" but follow your gut intuition and stay with it; even if it fails once or twice or three times, keep going.

I find that when you totally trust a new situation that people come your way, and this is what business people have told me. They've said that they've met people, sometimes their own colleagues, who have helped them to start something that they always wanted to do. Actually people help them much more than the mind gives credit to, when the trust is there, rather than when the fear is being experienced - people help, situations arise, and things fall into place.

This has happened to me many, many times to a point now that I don't even worry about anything, I just trust. I know things work out. But it's not the hippie sort of, lets just wait and see what happens. You have to actually take those steps.

You have to take action in a real sense.

Feel the intention, know the intention and move forward and not fear failing.

Chapter 17

People may criticize what you're doing and maybe you have to downsize and maybe all those luxuries that people say are important become difficult to maintain but somehow (I'm not saying just to simplify life) things fall into place.

My experience was that I said to my family, when I was much younger, that I had no intention to go and do what was expected to be my path in some people's eyes. I just wanted to travel and experience life in a way that is amazing and to open my mind in a different way than doing those normal things that I didn't feel would help me.

I had no money, no way of supporting myself and now twenty years later I'm still doing this, traveling and experiencing life and I'm writing books and I'm doing exactly what I want to do. And had I not gone through this journey that I write about in one of my books, I would never have been able to be where I am now.

The experiences form your whole life. You meet people and you have experiences.

For me, you live once and you might as well live completely and intensely and fully and not let fear stop you from taking those actions that need to be taken for you to live life in a way that makes you happy and free.

I conduct seminars and retreats rather than coaching people one-on one in order to work with many people, as there are many people that really need help right now. Generally in places that are beautiful, in nature, car free, industry free, pristine locations for those present to experience something (the beauty of nature) that may be lacking in their daily lives. The retreats and seminars are generally working with fear—letting go of the limitations of fear and seeing the wisdom behind them, seeing what is not really being understood, expressed and completely experienced.

Fear to me, is not negative. Fear is actually like anger. It is a communication that has a deeper message. Once we let go of the superficial, there is a deeper message that you can understand.

I would like to share with you a meditation that helps to bring us back to the consciousness that many have lost in our civilization. We have lost it as we have developed more and more into a society where everything is fast and everything is about impact rather than actually coming back home to oneself, coming back to the essence.

I would like you to take a few moments to practice this.

Close your eyes because by closing your eyes the senses relax a little bit more. It is good to sit up and good to have your back straight so that you're really focused on the conscious aspect of this meditation.

As you sit up and close your eyes, take a few moments to breathe in—the breath is very important. So don't just breathe in, in an automatic way, in a mechanical way. This is part of our attention moving always to the external aspects; even the breath then becomes external to you. So when you breathe in, what you are doing is you are bringing everything around you a little bit closer to you. Basically you are saying to yourself, "I allow my heart to feel more intimate with life. I allow my heart to be more vulnerable to the waves that come and go, that life is always creating around me, with no fear."

As you breathe in, it's impossible to feel fear. If you take a deep in-breath what you are doing is allowing the fear to move out of that space that occupies feelings. If you breathe in deeply what you are breathing in is a life force that is very vibrant. Breathe in deeply and then, as you breathe out, let go, breathe out, let go, and imagine that all those aspects of life that are swirling around in your mind, or that are occupying the space of the heart or that are occupying you, or stressing you or creating tension for you, imagine (imagination is very powerful), imagine that through the out-breath, the fearful aspects are moving out from your body, out from your feelings, out from your mind. It requires a little bit of discipline to do this because it's so easy to drift back into another thought, another feeling, another situation, another idea, another dream.

Rather than drift back, have the intention so clear that all that will happen now is that you are letting go and becoming a channel. Becoming an open vessel for the divine aspect that is inside of your heart. Let go of the mundane, no matter how important it is, no matter how practical those issues are that need to be dealt with. Give your heart a moment to deeply relax, to really come back to itself so that you are doing nothing, all you are doing is breathing in deeply again.

And, as you breathe in deeply, not trying to change anything, not trying to change the thoughts or the feelings, simply allowing the vibrancy of the in-breath to fill your body, what is happening is that you are helping the body move to a higher vibration, to a higher state of being. And this is the only possible way to change any situation around you. This is the way to move beyond it, not to be attached, not to be caught up, not to be stuck or limited by whatever life is throwing at you but rather to completely let go as you breathe in, to completely let go of everything except the gratitude of being alive, because all that counts is this moment. And this moment is your in-breath.

As you breathe in, everything else is of no importance because after the in-breath there is a moment between the in-breath and the outbreath where you can be still. And in that stillness there is an open space, there is a feeling that goes beyond human feelings. There is a deep, divine feeling that begins to bubble up from the depths into this wonderful being that is you. The human aspect that is you. And you begin to feel better.

This is how transformation happens. You transform through joy and happiness.

When we know that time is precious, when we know that life is precious, we utilize this gift in a very special way. We don't waste it; we don't create limitations around it. And that is the out-breath. We let go of whatever stops this feeling. We let go of the limiting negative emotions, of selfishness, of feeling insecure, lack of self-esteem, all of those human aspects that are important but that take us nowhere, let them go.

Take a few moments to bring your consciousness back to the area of the heart, the heart energy point. Feel this in the chest and realize that you are not alone, that by doing this action you are connecting to many, many conscious beings around you who at this moment are celebrating the divine, and you have just been invited to this celebration.

When you breathe in and out and feel good and there is happiness inside of your heart, you celebrate and you invite more people to this wonderful space that is ever expanding, As you move to this space of celebration, take a few moments to bring this awareness into your whole being so that the whole physiology of your body can begin to change.

This meditation takes just a few moments, and it changes much more than you may realize.

In every moment there is a choice. I believe that the world today is beautiful and I celebrate it totally, not with fear but with joy and happiness and a gratitude for being alive. This is what I ask people to consider experiencing now, in this moment.

Chapter 17

* * *

Tony Samara, author of 'Shaman's Wisdom,' 'From the Heart,' 'Different Yet the Same,' and 'Deeper than Words' was born in England, grew up in Egypt and also in Norway where he discovered the "Zen Buddhist philosophy". This discovery eventually led him to the "Mount Baldy Zen Center in California, USA" where he learned the spiritual teachings of "Kyozan Joshu Sasaki." He had curiosity to explore further the essence of spirituality and thus went to live and learn with shamanic communities around the globe. Now people from all over the world visit Tony Samara to take spiritual guidance and experience being in his presence. Tony believes that *"the vast majority of people go through life without directly experiencing the depths of their true self, or understanding their connection to life, or their relationship to others and to the world at large. We are often taught to only relate to the world through our senses. We think, we reason, we feel — but we do not know from our hearts what it means to be connected to what is beyond the senses."* He believes that direct experiences have the potential to radically transform an individual and his or her life, as well as promote a profound and effortless letting go of past emotional, mental and physical pain and suffering. His main countries of activity are in Europe, yet with the assistance of the Internet, is attracting a Global audience through frequent online interviews and live satsangs. His function is as a Spiritual Teacher who encourages all to lead their lives actively in a noble way in order to realize the evolution of human consciousness. Tony may be found at www.tonysamara.org

192

Benjamin Smythe

chapter 18

Benjamin Smythe

Unlost and Found

On a cold night in December of 2008, I stepped out onto the snow-covered deck, looked up at the stars, and whispered with total sincerity from the most exhausted place I had ever been . . .

"God?"

Absolutely nothing happened...and then everything answered: the stars, the trees, the wood, the space, the breath, the body, the thoughts, the emotions, the cold, the colors, the wind, etc. I cried and felt wave after wave of bliss and then I became very still and the next thing I knew it was now.

This is it. This is the answer. The answer never stops answering.

This.

It is so simple, there is no reward.
It is so obvious, there is no prize.

Everything is in motion. Whatever this is, it is already happening.

There is nothing to understand or figure out because what could be understood or figured out is already happening.

All feelings belong to the universe, including the feeling of something missing.

It does not answer to any name as it is all names possible.
It does not fear any fear, as it is all death possible.
It does not lose anything for everything that can be lost is found within it.

Even "it" cannot describe the simplicity that this is.
Even "this" and "is" are lies.

There is no true or false nature. There is simply Nature.
There is no seeking enlightenment.
There is no searching for the truth.
There is no journey home that is different than what is already happening.

Everything is already happening. Everything.

It is so obvious it leaves no hope, nor any need for hope.

This is so simple there is no achievement possible. This is so all inclusive seeking is a feeling finding is having.

This is it.

This is the unlost and found.

* * *

Benjamin Smythe, age 36, 6', 155 pounds, likes chicken burritos, graphic novels, skateboarding, Sandra, Wheel of Fortune, and Modern Family. When he is not home in Berkeley, California, he is traveling around sharing the impeccable simplicity of non-duality as is. For more information, please visit www.benjamintsmythe.com

Thornton Streeter, D.Sc.

Kimberly Schipke, M.S.

chapter 19

Thornton Streeter, D.Sc.
and Kimberly Schipke, M.S.

The Journey Home

Journey is a word which conjures up the feeling of movement and implies a length of time. When one voices the word "home," a completely different feeling is aroused. A feeling of peace and stillness pervades our being. So as the place where we lay our hat is our home, this home does not have to be an actual building. Home can be a metaphysical place in time and space where family, whether single unit or a group, is nourished and rests. This is important because our intuition and instincts are therefore pulsing to a different beat than that of our left-brain concerns of meeting the mortgage or rent payments on time every month. Home is certainly not a house where debt can cause more stress than the rest and nourishment gained. Home is our sanctuary from the world, yet in the world. It is therefore necessary for us to explore further what we mean by "journey" and what we mean by "home." In the journey below we will travel not just on a path but also through the dimensions of our being to explore if we are really manifesting our highest potential and the technologies used to monitor the human being while journeying.

Many ancient spiritual traditions are aware of the progression of an individual into higher states of consciousness, as many of their adepts have reached the highest level of consciousness where they can see and witness the terrain around them. The biofield has often been seen, described and depicted in religious and spiritual writings dating back to the earliest texts, as example of which is shown in Figure 1. Until the early 20th century, detection of the biofield remained in the hands of certain gifted individuals, including clairvoyants whose enhanced range of "sight" allowed them to detect energy fields through their visual cortex and a development of the more etheric "third eye" brow chakra. The biofield acts as a protective sheath which can be disturbed which leads to illness and disease as it is the matrix upon which our physical body is formed. Changes in the physical/emotional health of an individual are reflected and can thus be detected in their biofield. As we embark on our journey, we must first explore the lessons of our ancient roots.

Figure 1: Buddhist Tanka. Green highlights the crown and blue surrounds the body.

The layers of the Earth's atmosphere change according to gas composition, pressure, and temperature as it expands into gravity-free space. As the Earth's atmospheric layers are well proven, it is now time to explore the subtle changes in the layers of the human atmosphere as described in ancient writings (see Figure 2). It is widely recorded that there are seven interpenetrating layers of the biofield: (1)Etheric body, (2)Astral body, (3)Mental body, (4)Causal body, (5)Celestial body, (6)Ketheric body and (7)the Soul. The Khore, of the esoteric literature of the Zoroastrian tradition, describes nine layers of the human body as outlined below.

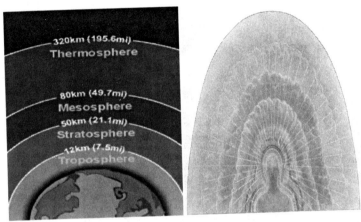

Figure 2: Depiction of the Earth's atmosphere and the human biofield

The first layer of the human body is the densest physical layer known as the skeleton. All organs, systems, muscles, flesh and skin comprise the second layer. The third is also a physical layer, an etheric, fluid-like substance that flows in and out of the skin. This layer is considered part of the physical biofield and plays the important role of removing the etheric toxins from the body. Toxins of high enough frequency that they are expelled directly through the skin via sweat and do not rely on either an excretory system, like the kidney, bladder, and urinary tract for liquids, or the intestines and bowels for solids. The fourth layer is known as the aura. The gross outline of the body's energy plexii or chakras is observed in this layer. The etheric field of the aura is the densest of all the energy bodies and is closely related to the physical. It is thought to extend up to 2 cm beyond the surface of the skin. The fifth layer represents life force carrying the physical gases, oxygen etc., and the vibrationary currents. This is also known as the mental body. The sixth or astral layer carries the emotional desires and the most intimate thoughts, which are translated through the Soul. The seventh layer is the nine light-layered soul that nestles in the heart chakra and is ultimately responsible for all physical, biological and chemical functions. The eighth layer is the celestial body and the spiritual awareness of the Divine Universal Natural Laws. This is the Soul's self-creating journey back to the Godhead and Stardom. The ninth layer, the Etheric body, is the spiritual connection of the Soul with the Godhead. Dennis Milner, in his book the "Loom of Creation", recounts his observations of distinct biofield layers with circular and triangular shapes of bio-photonic emissions at differing levels which gives evidence of subtle structure of light around the body.

The seven major chakras or energy centers are spinning vortices of energy in a spiral configuration similar to the spiral of the Milky Way galaxy. The chakras spin at their own specific frequencies with the slowest spinning chakra at the base and the highest at the crown. The chakras draw in energy from the universal energy field and then it is distributed via the meridians (channels) of the etheric body to the cells of the physical body. In human anatomy they are closely linked to endocrine glandular function and immunology. The spin of the chakras is caused by energy from neuronal excitation along the Vegas nerve and endocrine gland activity which produce changes in electrical activity and the subtle atmospheric changes due to hormonal changes. They are spinning vortices that open to absorb required solar and cosmic vibrations and also to eliminate etheric toxins. Each chakra or energy centre therefore acts as a transponder. The seven major Chakras account for the seven major musical notes, the seven colours of the rainbow, as well as seven states of consciousness related to the seven heavenly virtues and the seven deadly sins. Their function is to transmute lower frequencies into higher frequencies and vice-versa. Ultimately the body interacts with the cosmos through light to balance itself. The Vedas are scientific manuals for the structure and function of the chakras and nadis (meridians).

What is this layering of dimensional consciousness and why is it important? It is our journey home.

In the first dimension of consciousness, man is concerned with survival. This is the dimension of earth and many are disturbed on this level of consciousness because they are not grounded, often separated by a modern lifestyle of high rises, pavement and fast moving transport. The healing lesson is to reconnect with the Earth and stand barefoot on the grass with nothing between us. This allows for a discharge of static electricity and helps induce balance to electromagnetic properties of the biofield. An individual can live quite comfortably in the ignorant bliss of survival mode but somehow cut off from nature and unable to grow. The root or base chakra is a vortex of spiraling energy that is able to act as a satellite for absorbing geo-plasmic earth frequencies, or as an energy trap door for the most physical and slowest of the etheric toxins. In Sanskrit there are many sacred sound vibrations and Yantra configurations to help the devotee rebalance through vocalization/chanting and meditation. The colour often associated with this chakra is the slowest on the visible spectrum, red, and resonates with the musical note C. In one dimension a point exists with no frame of reference, so as the next dimension is established we can start being aware of those closest to us.

The second level of consciousness in mankind is found in the dimension of relationships. He becomes social and seeks to quench his thirst as this is the dimension of water and therefore of emotions. In order to keep exploring the dimensionality of ourselves, we find balance and peace at home, in our relationships and with our family. Many of us are quite content in this state of family bliss and there is no desire to experience life beyond the simple pleasures of home and family life. Until this is achieved there may always be a void that needs to be filled and nurtured. There is confusion about the naval chakra area, more than any other. The reason for this is that there are in fact several minor chakras. The Vedic tradition states that all major chakras are along the central spinal axis. Yet many other traditions have the major splenic chakra off-centre above the spleen. In our research the splenic chakra relates to the sex glands and is measured two finger widths below the navel. Otherwise known as the sacral or naval chakra that corresponds to the Hara of Chinese medicine. The note that resonates with this chakra is D and the colour is orange.

The third dimensional state of consciousness is where a family can transcend the "home" and become part of the wider community. Here we have an ancient association with the element "Fire". This is the literal fire of warmth and given off as energy that is consumed in cellular activity. Because of the link to fire, an intellectual individual can explore the burning questions in his mind. This is therefore the dimension of the "ego" and is concerned with the "I", the "me", and "the self". Many remain here in this third dimension fearful of the mystery of time (aging) and so pre-occupied with community and family survival that they are unaware of those levels above to even desire to rise to meet them. Man is concerned with nourishment and learns to save and store food for the winters. The solar plexus helps modern medical practitioners understand the concept of chakras because solar plexus is a term they often use and in a location they know. Its physiological function deals with digestion and is the chakra that is activated whenever the fire element is generated in the body. The note E and the colour yellow are associated with this Manipura chakra. Now we have integrated the three-dimensional "space" and our place in it, which carries our awareness to the next plane.

In the fourth dimension of life we have "time" and we are conscious of our heartbeat and breath and their rhythm. This is the dimension of the element air and we find mastery in this dimension by learning to really breathe. Here we have transcended the physicality of earth, water and fire and now soar with unconditional love to our destiny. If discord is present in this state we can become envious and acquisitive. Here unconditional love becomes a twisted heart and the bright green of healing becomes the murky green of envy, so our ever-present challenge is to love and be loved. The green governing colour of balance is associated with this chakra, yet like the Sun it can often appear like a golden yellow. The thymus gland and the note "F" are two other links.

In the 5th dimension of life we are all about expression and reception. We are communicating our knowing to others to share the insights of our experience. This is the dimension of etheric energy and it's element that scientists call "dark matter," because we do know it is the bridge to highest state of consciousness. The throat centre is associated with good communication skills when balanced, but can get twisted by frustration of not being heard and transform into arthritic tendencies or chronic fatigue. The throat chakra has two predominant colors, orange which stimulates the thyroid gland and triggers the expansion of the lungs, and indigo, which stimulates the parathyroid and triggers the contraction of the lungs. The colour blue and the element Akasha are associated with this gateway to the higher senses.

The sixth dimension of consciousness is our sense of knowing and in this state we connect with our intuition. At the brow, is a centre of energy that is also known as the "third eye," which of course implies seeing something. What can we see with this eye?

If it is open and the viewing faculty is well developed we can see the majesty of these higher dimensions as if a Shaman entranced with the holy vine. A master of this dimension is both telepathic and clairvoyant and understands what really is Space.

As we journey to this centre we experience flashes of intuition and wakefulness and this is where we seek our spiritual nourishment. If an individual gets disturbed at this level, he can become enmeshed in lust, lust for power and sexual gratification. An imbalanced signal on an etheric level stimulates the pituitary to release various hormones which allow the body to make the physiological adjustments as required. This is the same way traumas are stored in the body as physical disease.

The pituitary also has the most influence over the other major endocrine glands in the body. These glands on an energetic level are light flower buds and when activated by a signal from the pituitary in the form of a hormone, they open, and these etheric petals are chakras. The brow chakra has two petals, which reflects the duality of the mind.

In the seventh dimension, we have ascended to the apex of the head and are now at one with the universe. There is no separation and we are truly home. As this dimension is beyond time and space this is where we can experience healing at a distance from experienced practitioners, who with humility overcome any pride and with a clear awareness of the whole can help others on their journey transcending both belief and faith.

We have journeyed through all the virtues of man by mastering each dimension of consciousness, and in turn, we have transcended the labyrinth of deadly sins to reach the ultimate realization. We are now throbbing with a glow of biophotons, super-sensory to every taste, smell and feeling and these become a heavenly cascade of experiences.

Now possessed by the ultimate consciousness we are humbled by the grace and empowered to share this holiness with others. The crown chakra is located at the vertex and is known as the 'thousand petal lotus'. It is the spiritual link of the individual soul with the rest of existence and when we all realize this, we are all home.

There are also 16 minor chakras that exist in such places as the back of the knees, base of the feet, palms of the hands and in the eyes, to name a few. Interestingly these charkas link with the other more major ones. Such an example is the manner with which the palm chakras connect directly to the heart chakra, which explains how the majority of healing operates through the laying on of hands.

In actuality there are as many energy vortices (chakras) as there are pores in the body, however energy passed directly to the major charkas is obviously a more efficient method of affecting the energy systems.

There are differing allocations concerning the crown and brow energy centers and the pituitary and pineal glands. In fact almost half of the relevant literature relates the pineal to the crown while the other half relates it to the brow centre.

As the master gland the pituitary influences the function of many of the other glands, this should clearly indicate its association with the crown chakra. In the same way the pineal gland with cells similar to the optic cells would lend itself to being associated with the brow centre ("third eye" chakra). The crown chakra is situated on the top of the head in some individuals. In others it can be found in the area of the vertex. The base chakra is located around the perineum.

In the male the epicentre for the base is located more to the front of the body, corresponding to the position of the prostate. In the female it is configured more towards the back of the body, corresponding to the cervix. The back of the chakra is opposite the front for the throat, heart, solar plexus and navel chakras.

The position of the chakras can vary slightly from individual to individual (e.g. the heart chakra may be found a little to the left or right of the midline in some people. It may be the case that the chakra front and back may exist upon an angle and not travel through the body in a level line.

For example, the heart chakra may be lower on the front of the body and higher on the back. In disease states the chakra may be seen to deviate from its normal healthy position (i.e. energy flows may be so disrupted that the chakra is unable to maintain its normal position).

Based on such concepts, there now exists a whole body of medicine termed "energy" or "vibrational medicine". This approach acknowledges the non-physical (subtle energetic) make-up of the body and seeks to treat disease by releasing energy blockages and imbalances. In turn, this helps to rebalance and sustain the physical/emotional body's health.

It is the case that when a broken bone is left it will eventually heal itself leaving no pain, but with limited durability, mobility and strength. However, if the bone is repositioned to set in the correct manor then full durability, mobility and strength can return. The same is true with the biofield. Any damage to the physical/emotional system will be reflective of a corresponding weakness in the biofield. If no attention is given to the underlying energy matrix then any repairs carried out on the physical/emotional body will be done upon an unsound energy matrix and thus have limited durability, mobility and strength.

According to John White's global research, the human biofield is a common denominator in up to 97 different individual cultures from Ancient Egypt to South American Shamanism, each with their own specific vocabulary; this makes it one of most consistent dimensions of all human understanding. The electromagnetic radiations surrounding a human being can now be measured with a variety of different devices, such as the Medical Thermal Imaging, Polycontrast Interference Photography (PIP), Kirlian Photgraphy, and Electro Photonic Imaging (EPI).

"An ability to detect illness and energetic disturbances reliably and accurately in a person's etheric body days or weeks prior to the appearance of actual physical symptoms would be truly miraculous" ~ (Richard Gerber, 2000)

It is important to continue the development of a toolbox of safe, efficient, and cost-effective techniques to help assist the primary healthcare worker and the integrated clinical team in evaluating or triangulating an individual's health trajectory. The Health Trajectory (HT) is a method of mapping an individual health status, both now and in the future, against an average peer group norm.

There is a model of disease stages based on seven distinct stages of manifestation. These different levels are measured against an axis of time and are sub-divided from three major groups: pre-medical, medical and post-medical. The Atlas of Disease States is composed of a series of biofield images and data collated to reveal the stages of each disease state to triangulate an individual's health trajectory.

Primary pre-symptomatic is the first stage of disease manifestation and can be seen as congestion or a leak in the meridians or energy channels. The acupuncture points therefore reveal this primary stage long before the individual feels any pain, hence the tradition in China where the community paid the doctors to keep them healthy and were reimbursed when taken ill.

Secondary pre-symptomatic occurs when the imbalance affects the chakras in the biofield, which disrupts the body's natural self-healing mechanism.

Primary symptomatic is the stage where the patient feels discomfort. The biofield will now reveal imbalances not just in the meridians and chakras but also in the entire system as the disease takes its physical manifestation. Earliest pathological test would now reveal this imbalance.

Secondary symptomatic occurs when a person feels pain and decides to go to the doctor. Symptoms now reveal an advanced stage of the disease when it is more difficult to address and doctors are contacted for consultation.

Acute conditions vary and a number of different assessment techniques are required to identify the exact nature of the issue. This is expensive and time consuming and can often have a huge economic impact on all those concerned.

Chronic illness is well mapped by modern scanners such and CAT scan, MRI, and ultrasound, but it is often stated that modern medicine does not have all the answers as far as treating chronic disease.

Terminal cases can in rare circumstances experience a remission and there are amazing stories of remissions often linked to a positive outlook and a desire to first understand and then lift the imbalance back into equilibrium.

This model of disease onset allows the practitioner to compare any patient's biofield profile with a database of others recordings. The individual screened is compared to other individuals with known pathology using a range of different analysis techniques such as pattern recognition and size averaging. Consistencies between scanning devices and medical records will be recorded for future database comparisons.

In order to triangulate an individual's health trajectory it is important to have data from the widest possible spectrum. If this data can be collected cheaply, quickly and non-invasively, then this is so much the better. Medical thermal imaging, Electro-Photonic Imaging and PIP biofield imaging represent medical research tools which investigate the biofield and in total represent over 150 years of research and thousands of published papers.

The infrared spectrum lies between 2500 to 1600nm or 1.9e13 to 1.2e14Hz and represents the thermal radiations within the electromagnetic spectrum. With respect to the human biofield, the infrared spectrum shows the heat radiating from the body, which is outside of the visible spectrum. Body heat can be felt inches away from the skin's surface, which allows scientists to recognize that thermal energy is part of the human biofield.

Initially, thermal imagers were used in research, which only showed a temperature pattern but were not calibrated to measure specific temperatures. Recently, military-grade radiometric cameras which measure the absolute skin surface temperature have become affordable for medical use. Pixel resolution has also improved which provides high-definition, radiometric images to now be used to further validate the use of medical thermal imaging for preventative screening with quantitative thermal analysis.

According to the National Heart, Lung, and Blood Institute (United States), nearly half of the people who suffer heart attacks each year have what doctors refer to as "normal" cholesterol and many of those who died from heart attacks were later discovered by autopsy to have small cholesterol plaques. Inflammation agitates small plaques and causes them to become unstable, which makes them more likely to rupture than large plaques. Often times if the blood work comes back normal and blood vessel diameter is normal based on echocardiogram, and no treatment is given.

Thermal imaging allows practitioners to identify if inflammation is located in the carotid arteries, which run along the neck and bring oxygen to the brain. If inflammation is observed in these areas (see Figure 3) it is an early indicator of heart disease.

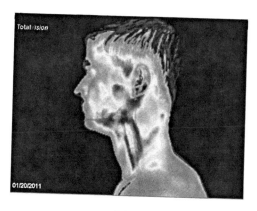

Figure 3: Photo taken with TotalVision software showing the overlay of the carotid artery along the neck and jaw. Note: Linear hyperthermic pattern on the neck. (*Image Courtesy of SafeScan Inc. www.safescaninc.com*)

Over the past two years in the United States there has been mixed recommendations regarding the relevance of medical thermal imaging for breast cancer detection. The basic principle behind the use of the technology is simple. A tumor typically outgrows the surrounding vasculature and requires a new blood supply. The neovascularization of breast tumors can be detected by medical thermal imaging years before a mammogram, as on average a tumor will live inside a woman's breast for 8 years before it is large enough to be detected by the human eye with the use of mammography.

The high metabolic activity of the tumor can be monitored as the heat reaches the skin's surface and produces an asymmetry. Figure 4 shows the reverse grey scale image of a woman with cancer in her left breast. As there is no radiation, multiple images at various angles can be taken to view the entire breast rather than limited to a particular area or type of tissue.

An additional benefit is providing a method of screening women with breast implants without the potential of causing rupture and doctors can monitor for inflammation if rupture occurs.

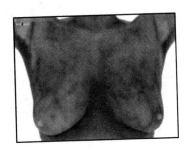

Figure 4: Neovascularization of breast cancer in the right breast, which spread to the left.

Medical thermal imaging allows practitioners to map the weather patterns of the body to address areas out of thermal equilibrium to restore balance and symmetry to the thermal radiations of the body. It is a useful tool for therapies such as acupuncture, reiki, massage, pranic healing, etc., which work on the energetic level.

Figure 5 is a progression of pictures of an acupuncture treatment for inflammation in the knee. Pictures are taken every five minutes for 30 minutes and both the practitioner and the client can see the effectiveness of the treatment. It also allows the patient to see that although there was improvement, there are still a few areas which may still need attention and will thus be more compliant to return for further treatment.

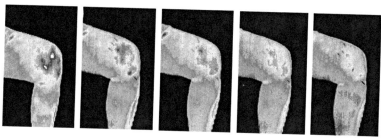

Figure 5: Acupuncture treatment over a span of 30 minutes/ (*Images courtesy of Dr. Carol Chandler of MyLife Imaging*)

Thin filaments referred to as Bonghan ducts were discovered by Professor Soh at Seoul University using modern dissection techniques. These ducts have been discovered within the cardiovascular and lymphatic systems and are also said to create "webs" around the organs, seen in Figure 6.

Bonghan ducts could possibly explain the meridians and nadis referred to in ancient Chinese and Vedic literature. Research scientists in Germany used moxibustion, the application of heat to an acupuncture point, and captured thin lines of thermal activity along the associated meridian by medical thermal imaging in Figure 7.

A map of the energy flow through the body can now be created rather than drawing the reported locations of meridians on a picture of the human body.

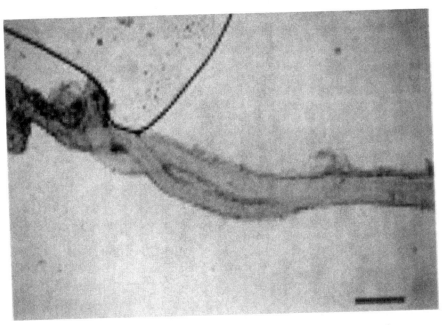

Figure 6: Bonghan duct extracted from a blood vessel

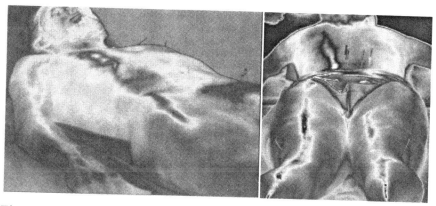

Figure 7: Moxibustion of the stomach (left) and bladder (right) meridians

The concept of universal energy is the most common theme of all mystical traditions. In TOM the term chi or qi is used to describe its presence. In terms of human anatomy the chi is the bio-energy and, in its multiple forms, it provides the breath of life. There is the division between genetic chi and inherited chi that both reside in the kidneys, and with splenic chi that derives its energy from food, breath and the environment.

The acupuncture points are the link between the chakra system, as they are mini-chakras themselves, and stimulate/release the flow of chi along the meridians. These points are not in dispute as they are being stimulated, needled and monitored by millions throughout the world and have been fixed, stained, and viewed under microscopy as shown in Figure 8.

A new device called the Acuview-4 is currently being marketed which claims to visualise the points and reveal their exact location and functional health, see Figure 8. By stimulating the body with the use of crystals, these acupuncture points begin to glow.

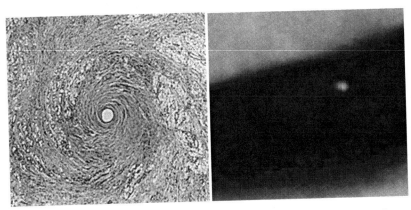

Figure 8: (Left) Fixed tissue embedded stained microscopic view of an acupuncture point; (Right) Acupuncture point illuminated by the Acuview-4

There is a difference of up to 70,000 Ohms between the skin's resistance on an acu-point than on any another part of the skin surface. Galvanic skin response devices are often used to measure the electrical activity of acupuncture points to help assist in diagnosing the health status of a person. The acu-points can be divided into several groups, primary points, confluent points, connecting points and cleft points. Further sub-divisions are back-shu points, front-mu points, crossing points, influential points, and auricular points.

Their original Chinese names also reveal their purpose, well points, spring points, stream points, river points and sea points. Others are named after animals, such as fish and rabbit; plants such as bamboo; objects such as cooking vessel and basin and architectural structures, such as gate, window, chimney, courtyard and platform.

The Ashi points are "unfixed points" and tender spots as they are not anatomically standardized and appear nameless but are used especially in pain relief. The biofield is therefore being emitted from the body by thousands of tiny flash lights, and combined they comprise the elliptical sheath referred to as the human biofield. Electro-Photonic Imaging measures the gas discharge/light emitted from the acupuncture points on the fingertips to give insight into the health status of the meridians.

Russian scientist, Konstantin Korotkov, invented Gas Discharge Visualization which is now referred to as Electro Photonic Imaging. The device is based on Kirlian photography which measures the gas/light emissions from biological systems. Each fingertip is placed on the surface of a quartz plate, which is then stimulated with a small electric charge, which stimulates the release of gas and biophotons via the dielectric effect.

The light captured from the acupuncture point is then used in analysis of body function as based on the Su Jok meridian system, shown in Figure 9. Over 750 research papers have been published involving EPI and it is registered as a medical device in Russia.

The EPI has developed software to such an extent that it bridges the live information measured from the finger tips and translate it into a language that modern medical professionals can understand, relate and integrate the information gleaned into their prognosis.

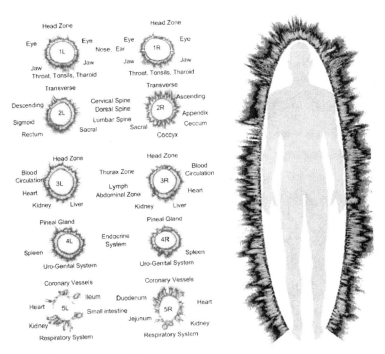

Figure 9: Su Jok meridian system used in EPI analysis (Left); Biofield composite (Right)

Over the past century a number of systems have been developed which attempt to detect aspects of the biofield. Although the mechanism of each device varies often they rely on an interactive process with the revealed data or image being a result of this interaction.

One of the first to provide visual evidence of subtle energies and biofields were Semyon and Valerie Kirlian with their now well-publicized Phantom Leaf experiments in the 1940s (Gerber, Vibrational Medicine, 2000).

In the modern era, a number of systems available including advanced forms of Kirlian, which are able to visualize and/or quantify the biofield. Polycontrast Interference Photography (PIP) does have similarities to Kirlian in that it provides an "indirect" interpretation of the biofield. With the creation of a Kirlian photograph the image is produced by electrical discharge and therefore the body has to be stimulated; however, with PIP the image is a visualization of light photon interactions with the subtle energies of the biofield.

This has the advantage of eliminating the impact of artifact such as moisture of the hand when carrying out assessments, which a common complaint made of Kirlian photography.

The PIP biofield imaging system detects the continuously exchanging energies between the subject under examination and its surrounding environment and forms interference patterns on and around its body with the incident rays from the light source, which means it is basically a light meter measuring light intensities. The energies captured by PIP are electromagnetic and include both visible and invisible ranges.

Electromagnetic energies have a strange property in that they do not appear to require any medium through which to travel. Some people thought that these fields were modifications of the subtle medium, or ether.

The human biofield might possibly interact with photons, "energy packets of light," sometimes called 'subtle energy photons'. Ambient (surrounding) light interacts with the field both when the incident ray travels toward the object and when the reflected ray bounces off the object. There are two mechanisms in physics whereby electric and magnetic fields affect photons.

The Faraday effect entails the rotation of polarized light in magnetic fields. The Kerr effect describes a similar effect with regard to electric fields. From analyzing these two statements, it is clear that these fields influence light. Light striking the physical body may be absorbed, or reflected. However, interaction with the non-physical aspects of the subject viewed with PIP is an interference phenomenon.

The effect of two energy healers working on an elderly man is shown in Figure 10 and over time a golden light emanates from and increases around the crown. An unknown physical phenomenon is occurring which involves the influencing of reflected light by the physical (and/or energetic) state of the human body. Quite how this occurs is open to conjecture, and Oldfield is not short of a few of his own explanations, but the most probable explanation involves the tenuous ionic discharge that takes place at the surface of the skin.

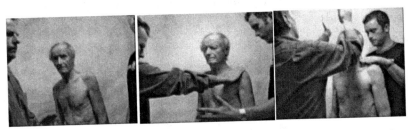

Figure 10: Hands on and hands off healing as revealed by PIP

One of our most significant discoveries is that when PIP image is taken out of focus, the camera settings more clearly reveals the functional health of the chakras as well as the overall human biofield.

An example can be seen in Figure 11 where a pool of sluggish energy or shielding at the heart chakra is observed which shows lack of one's ability to express emotions. The solar plexus chakra is open and active revealing an important self-healing mechanism.

When the body's endocrine system is out of harmony through excess workload or under activity, then the chakra emerges, like a water spout which forces currents of energy down the corresponding meridians and draws sluggish energy out of the biofield under pressure.

If an area is balanced and in harmony, one colour will predominate. Colors may be coherent, vibrant, bright, and vivid when an individual is healthy and speckled, dissipated, muddied, smudged, and dull when an individual is unhealthy. On a cellular level, the same contrast techniques can be applied to a microscope for observation of the range of vitality.

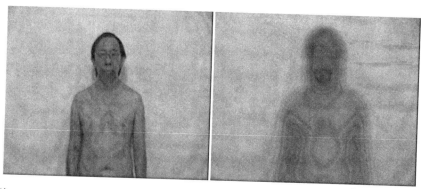

Figure 11: (Left) In-focus PIP of a 50+ year old male; (Right) Out-of-focus images which clearly reveals brow, throat, congested heart, solar and top of the splenic chakras.

With a detailed, scientific understanding of the human biofield, the current established principals of medicine from each tradition would be fully integrated and will assist in crossing the chasm between natural health prevention, remedies and treatments along with the allopathic models and techniques.

The objective of a modern healthcare system must be to provide a safe, effective and integrated approach to diagnosis and treatment with information about an individual's well-being on all levels: physical, mental, emotional, and spiritual.

These biofield devices when calibrated with FDA certified, non-invasive technologies such as medical thermal imaging which enable the integrated therapist to identify the root cause of disease and therefore the most precise treatment to restore health.

By measuring energetic interactions in the biofield, the integrated practitioner can bring forward his assessment of an individual's health trajectory and the mutation point from biofield imbalance to physiological disease.

Our journey home is now aided by predictive and preventative screening, with a new understanding of healing and healthy medicine. When we write scientifically about 'dimensions' we are talking about dimensions of consciousness and in this journey we are now familiar with at least 7 of them, not just the 3 dimensions of space plus time. We need this to realize our higher potential, and instead of environmental annihilation, work towards recreating heaven on earth - a new Eden for now.

* * *

Dr. Thornton Streeter DSc. is a special Advisor to the ICNM, the UK's leading authority on Complementary and Natural Medicine and as a faculty member of Zoroastrian College's Holistic Health Department has been invited to promote their NGO Status with the UN and have his training programs recognized in 190 countries. He is Director of The Centre for Biofield Sciences based in the UK with a branch in India. He has spent over fifteen years specializing on researching the Human biofield. Dr. Streeter is one of the few certified trainers of Polycontrast Interference Photography (PIP). He is also a qualified Electro Crystal Therapist (EleCT). Dr. Streeter has overseen the development of a uniquely recognized & officially approved PIP training program. www.pipbiofieldimaging.com. For more information, please visit www.biofieldsciences.com, www.biofieldscience.org

Kimberly Schipke, M.S., C.C.T. is a biomedical engineer with over six years of research experience in tissue engineering, cellular/tissue mechanobiology, and medical device design. She is adept in the rules and regulations of the Food and Drug Administration as well as the Department for Health and Human Services. She is a certified clinical thermographer and trainer in medical thermal imaging to help scientists develop protocols for quantifying thermal energetic changes in the body with various bioenergetic devices and techniques. She may be reached at kimberly.schipke@gmail.com and www.safescaninc.com

Thornton and Kimberly have an extensive list of published works.

chapter 20

David W. Taylor

Prayer to Amma

Glimpsing the truth of
"There really is no loss"
Like an Instamatic flash throughout
My viscera
I still grieve intangible things.

I still fanaticize of surrendering
All of my boundaries in a voluptuous
Aubergine night,
I still dream for long lingering evenings
Filled with the Amber light of laughter
And song,
I still imagine days of blessings granted
Out of a Cerulean sky.

And yet,
While looking at a photograph of the Ocean
Taken from a height where the air is
Finer than faith,
I am terrified of falling,
And surviving the impact
To discover that I can
Submerge to Indigo depths

And still breathe.

Don't tell me of Secrets and Mysteries,
I find I already know their anticlimactic
Answers.
But look upon me as I sleep and
In a golden whisper
Tell me again, the story of when we first met,
Tell me this in the language I've forgotten,
The language of my birth eons ago.

In my waking let my first sight be of your
Iridescent gaze,
That banishes the Umber taproot of doubt,
And remember – irrevocably,
Your love for me,
And the vivid strength it allows me.

* * *

David W. Taylor expresses himself as an Actor, Kitchen Designer/Salesman, Web Site Proprietor, Workshop Teacher, Public Speaker, Father, Son, Brother and occasionally as Writer. He currently resides in Austin, Texas the fact of which still blows his mind. He can be found at www.forgivenessinthemoment.com

John Troy

chapter 21

John Troy

Truth is Not a Thought

Truth is non-physical existence; not mortal existence. Some refer to that as Heart as that expression is headless and thoughtless. The "I am the body notion" is false; a belief. It never was. That includes the biological mind along with its offspring, thoughts. Truth is immaculate sentience that cannot be remembered by the insentient linear mind and is silent, seamless and still. The word, Truth, is a pointer only to the thoughtless Truth. Truth is Silent. Silence is the language of sentience. Silence makes no claim of its own, however Silence is the still, host "screen" the movie of daydreams is seen within. The movie is not what it seems to be. Attachment to a character or situation in the movie or dream carries with it carnal fear and reactive behavior. Truth is revealed by Grace as what one always already IS, prior to the dream and doership. As seeking is exhausted, Truth dawns and without a doer.

Consider the word, water. Is the very word, water, itself, wet? Can that word, itself, quench thirst? Is the word, water, really water? Of course it's not. It's just a word, a thought, not real water. It only refers to water which itself makes no claim of its own.

Now consider the word, "I". Is the word or even the internal assumption, "I", habitually arising in your head really who or what you are? Again, of course not; it is only an assumption, a thought, a letter in the alphabet that refers to the silent speechless state that is aware of I-word that reflects the silent sentience. The silent sentience, not the statement, I, is what you really are. Truth is not a thought.

Wisdom cannot be uttered, known, contained or found. That's because knowledge is comprised of insentient thoughts of the mind; a knower and a known. Wisdom is prior to any movement of the mind. Dwell in Wisdom, the thoughtless domicile of the wise as the primacy of being.

The mind and its I-thought are not the proper tools for Self discovery. Silent Sentience is the girder in the bridge to wisdom. Wisdom is not knowledge. Knowledge is always gained anew by the biological knower I-thought, called the mind; one thought tied to another to create a bundle of thoughts that in turn create a story-line from birth to death that defines an illusionary entity inherently dualistic. What is gained anew will certainly disappear eventually.

Conversely, Wisdom is empty, transparent and eternal stillness. Wisdom is birth-less and death-less, having no form. Knowledge is but a veneer of alphabets and concepts projected into reality to the point of distraction. It is learned ignorance. Release attention on the veneer of thoughts and allow free attention to reveal the true Self of sentient being without the I-thought and its offspring of thoughts obstructing native vision. This is the dawn and discovery of Wisdom; the heart of sentience and the domicile of the wise, Truth.

The building blocks of this illusion or the mortal paradigm are thoughts; words, concepts, beliefs, imagination, relationships, distraction and alphabets.

Thoughts and words have countless meanings which breed even more words that divide and breed even far more words; all divisive. Where will thinking end? Soon the ever growing bundle of thoughts becomes rather large like someone who collects pieces of string their whole life and connects each and every newfound piece found to the end of the ever-growing ball of string. Its gravity of never ending bifurcating knowledge commands and distracts native attention.

Herein this maze is the home of the imaginary ego-Narrator "I-thought." This I-thought can no more change the outcome of your life than a narrator describing a sports event can change the outcome of the game. It is only a belief; an illusion; a phantom; a second guesser.

The substratum of the mind is a foundation of silent sentience (like awake deep dreamless sleep), not a statement, but a thoughtless eternal, ever present sentience that is cognizant of the "I" and it's bundle of thoughts as well as when the I-thought is missing. This silent, still sentience is what you really are; the Truth. This still sentience is like a movie screen that the entire movie of life is viewed upon and within. It is the actual Here and Now your thoughts manifest and dissolve within (If it moves, it's the movie. No exception).

It is Wisdom. It is not dependent on the thoughts as knowledge. It does not require a diploma or the nod of a guru. It does not require religion or a school of thought. Wisdom is simple being or sentience prior to knowledge. Take rest in Wisdom prior to the mind and its imaginings.

There is no need to believe anything. Beliefs are thoughts. Always reserve the right to change one's mind. Beliefs are stubborn, closed minded, divisive and have an imaginary believer, equally another belief.

Beliefs are of the individual mind and constructed from words, thoughts and concepts rooted in the idea of mortal existence and the imaginary I-thought that inhabits and efforts the bundle of thoughts. Belief, time, space, distance and memory are thought-threads in the tapestry of illusion and that includes reincarnation, myths, religions, theologies, ideas and the like. The I-thought is a belief. Good is a belief. Evil is even a belief. Heaven is a belief. Hell is a belief. All after-life scenarios are beliefs. God is a belief. Enlightenment is a belief. Who you think you are is a belief. Each one is just another thought-thread woven in the tapestry of the illusory storyline of the mortal Myth.

Truth is Not a Thought.

* * *

John Troy can be found at www.thewizardllc.com

chapter 22

Vicki Woodyard

The Limbo of Letting Go

I am up in the middle of the night, urged out of bed by a phrase that popped into my head—the limbo of letting go—and now this phrase has me wide awake. I can see an old broom in my mind and can see myself going lower and lower as I struggle to get underneath the broom. Is this not what our journey through life is about?

Society tells us that we must leap over the worldly hurdles of life, vaulting our way to success, but I have found the opposite to be true. God has seen to it that I have learned more by going lower than I ever have by going higher. The ego is hell-bent on leaping higher, but what does it know?

Of course the word *limbo* also means being in a state of uncertainty, which is where faith is born. One needs no faith in the sun when it is out; only in the darkness do we need faith in the light. Letting go of certainty is a wisdom we are loathe to practice.

If I told you that losing a child to cancer brought me so low that I found God, you would have no trouble believing me. If I told you that it made me no happier, would you believe that, too? God is not about making you happy. He is about making you whole. That He would do whatever it takes for this to happen is the cosmic joke and the final truth.

Wholeness ultimately is the happiest place to be, but we struggle with this for years and years. At least I did. You see, wholeness means that you must reconcile your abject cowardice with your most magnificent courage. You must balance your weak points with your God-given talents, limbo-ing under the broom of the opposites.

When I see someone doing the limbo in my mind's eye, there is usually a crowd of onlookers clapping and cheering as you see how low you can go. Does this not parallel humility in the face of our daily challenges? Water seeks the lowest spot and we are the ocean.

Cancer has been a dominant theme in my life. Not mine, but my daughter's, who got it at the age of three and now my husband's. I have seen God holding out the broom and telling me to go lower on many different occasions. There was no clapping crowd, just me and an old broom of crisis. Can you go under chemo, surgery and radiation? How about death, grief and living in the absence of a beloved child? Go lower. Let go. Limbo lower now.

Letting go is easy when you realize that God is holding the broom, when you see that the God within is up to the challenge that letting go requires. For limbo is not forever, although it may seem that way.

I think that letting go requires only one thing, wholeness. And I am going to tell you how to get there immediately. Choose it. Choose heart over head, humility over height, and you will be healed by a higher power than the mind.

Hannah Hurnard wrote a spiritual classic called *Hinds' Feet On High Places.* It is about the journey of a character called Little Much Afraid. She sets out on the journey to the high places, called by The Good Shepherd. Only He doesn't seem so good to her when He asks that she learn to give love instead of seek it from others. He seems willing to sacrifice her very life for Him. But she begins her journey. He tells her to hold the hands of Sorrow and Suffering, two mysterious women who will help her on the journey.

When Little Much Afraid gets to the High Places, she has been promised a new name and that spurs her on. Ultimately after many challenges she reaches them, only to find that she must cast herself down from the very heights that she has taken such trouble to ascend. She must limbo lower now, as the musical phrase commands.

Of course, she finds that in going lower, she fulfills the purpose of her life—to serve instead of seek the high places. It is a journey of paradox and purpose. It is our journey. When will we go lower by own choice and not have it forced from us?

I am not talking about humiliation; I am talking about humility. Isn't letting go a form of humility? And yes, we will be forced to do what we do not choose consciously. That is how the game of life is played.

Maurice Nicoll, author of *Psychological Commentaries On The Teaching of Gurdjieff and Ouspensky,* was a great believer in willingness. He said if you go to something willingly, you win.

Choose to go lower, instead of higher. The mysterious limbo broom can heal you of unseen arrogance and many other negativities.

Often God only talks to us when He gets us so low that we are willing to listen. Cancer often brings us to this point, as do many other life-threatening situations. Will we have the faith to live in limbo, letting go and going lower? Because God never breaks a promise to His children. "Though He slay me, yet will I trust Him" (Job 13:15).

Victory is assured when we choose humility over the ego's height. You can't think your way into wholeness; you will be broken in the attempt. Schizophrenic thinking was never meant to heal a broken heart.

These days my heart is being challenged by cancer for the second time in my life. I am honoring the old broom of limbo. Will the battle against cancer be won or lost? That is a wrong question and I am going to suggest a right one. Will the limbo take me lower than I want to go? Of course, it always does, but I know Who is holding the broom.

* * *

Vicki Woodyard is the author of *Life With A Hole in It: That's How the Light Gets In* and *A Guru in the Guest Room*. She lives in Atlanta, Georgia. Her essays have been featured in many e-zines and her web site is popular with spiritual seekers all over the world. Please visit www.vickiwoodyard.com for more of Vicki's work; her books are available on www.amazon.com

Photo by Marc J Chalifoux | ChalifouxProcktor Photography | www.chalifouxprocktor.com

Keith Christian Wyatt

chapter 23

Keith Christian Wyatt

2012 The Journey Home

Shifting Perspectives

As the wheels of time turn, Ages come and go. And in their passing all that once flourished, and was familiar, gives way to that which is fresh, new, and unfathomable; until eventually, that too becomes familiar, and then forgotten, as the cycle continues and the Age turns again.

And though these cycles of birth, life, death and rebirth may give the impression that history is simply repeating itself; there are many today who sense that a quickening has begun; and that with it, it will bring unprecedented change.

This acceleration is marked by the increasing intensity of global events and by the rising temperature of nearly *every* planet in our solar system; while here on Earth, Time, itself, seems to be speeding up, and chaos mounting, as phenomenal shifts occur in our physical and perceptual realities with increasing rapidity.

This event, which many ancient cultures have prophetically termed "The Shift of Ages" has begun, and it is the final leg of our long Journey Home... back to One.

For it is commonly understood both in the realms of science and spirituality, that everything has come from One, and that to One we shall return. And even though the conflicts caused by humanity's struggle to attain for the self, at the expense of the Earth and all living things, seems to have brought the planet as far from oneness as it is possible to get; it is possible that our return to one may be as easy as making a simple shift in perspective. For it is the power that perspective has to awaken one to a new reality, that is reflected in the familiar phrase, "in order to change the world... one has only to change their mind."

Thus, if one is able to consider that everything has come from one, just as all the stars and galaxies of the universe are the product of one Big Bang; then one may see that since we have all come from the same source, we have actually always been, and will always be... one. And when one learns to see that we are *always* One, then one might also learn to see that the only thing that separates us from our oneness with everything, is our belief that we are separate.

Thus, the Journey Home back to One, is the soul's journey through countless lives and experiences, whose challenges and triumphs exist solely to urge the traveler to remember their oneness with all. And there are those who believe that the truth of our Oneness is never so easy to see as it is during the accelerated events that occur during The Shift of the Ages... and the birth of a new world.

But what is this shift? And how could it possibly result in the birth of a new world... and humanity's return to One? To answer these questions, one might consider some of the popular perspectives concerning 'The Shift' and the phenomenal opportunities that it presents to every soul on Earth during these days of great change.

Though one of the more popular perspectives views 'The Shift' as some grand event that is going to occur in the OUTER physical world, or in the cosmos, at some point between now and

Chapter 23

December 21, 2012 - bringing either salvation or destruction to the world—there are others who believe that "The Shift" is happening right now, and in fact, that it has been, and will always be happening.

These people believe that "The shift" can be experienced at any moment by anyone, who is willing to make The INNER Shift of Perspective back to One; where instead of seeing all beings and events of the world as separate and chaotic, the seeker learns to see that every aspect of existence is serving the Divine Plan by urging humanity to reestablish its faith and connection with the Divine Original Source of creation, known to many as God, or Great Spirit.

However today, many people's thoughts and awareness have moved about as far from One as it is possible to get; as humanity's dualistic perspective, and "survival of the fittest" mentalities, have served to divide the world into dueling pairs of opposites where many believe that they are "good" while others are "evil", that they are "light" while others are "dark", and that they are "right" while others are "wrong."

As a result, this divided perspective of existence has every human living for themselves, operating by his own Personal Will in an attempt to find INNER peace by shaping the OUTER WORLD according to his own likes and dislikes. However what so many people are realizing today is that the peace we seek cannot be found by creating change in the world OUTSIDE oneself, for true peace can only be found within.

And the moment one stops seeking outside oneself for peace, and starts looking within, is the moment one takes their first step on the long Journey Home… back to One. And we may see the truth of this when we consider that all around the world there are nearly 7 billion people who are trying to affect change in the world

OUTSIDE of themselves, in order to make others, and the world, match their vision of what is 'right', so that they can then find peace INSIDE.

However, when we realize that there are 7 billion people, with 7 billion different visions of what the world should look like; then we may see that that peace we seek can never be attained by trying to shape the physical world according to our dualistic ideals of "right" and "wrong"; as our conflicting views will always result in the paradoxical need to "fight for peace." Thus we may see that the only way to find TRUE everlasting PEACE, is to learn to be at peace with the way things are.

And though finding a way to be at peace with whatever comes in one's life may seem easier said than done, there are those who have experienced that such a feat can be attained by simply shifting one's perspective from the material... to the spiritual. This INNER shift occurs when one stops placing all importance on the struggle and seeming separation of the *physical* world, and learns to see the essential *spiritual* purpose that is served by everything in existence, including life's strife and conflicts.

For when one learns to see that all beings and events are serving the spirit, by encouraging us towards love's higher planes of compassion and forgiveness; then may one come to see that we could not reach the highest heights without facing and learning to love the darkest depths. And when one realizes that we need the physical trials and tribulations of life, to help us reach our spiritual potential, then may one learn to face all that comes in life with peace and gratitude.

For truly, it is the Darkness that inspires one to seek the Light; and as one realizes that the darkness of their life has played a part in making them who they are, by inspiring them towards a greater love for all, then might they learn to see that in fact that darkness is a part of them. And when one is able to consider their Oneness with the darkest parts of themselves and the world, then might they learn to see their Oneness with all that is; thus bringing them closer to the completion of their long Journey back to One.

And though the road home is long and fraught with challenge, Faith is the steadfast friend who will support the weary traveler on her journey back to one. For when one has faith that all beings and events exist for the Divine Purpose of encouraging us to seek and find that eternal peace INSIDE, then may they learn to see that all is in fact serving the divine, and therefore All IS divine.

And by thus establishing Faith that every event that happens in one's life occurs to assist their soul's evolution, one may come to see that Heaven is not a person, place or prize... it is a state of mind. For it is in this faithful state, and the love that accompanies it, that one is able to face and flow through all of life's challenges with grace and gratitude. And it is this ability to SEE ALL AS ONE, and all as DIVINE, that marks the individual's Inner Shift and Return to One.

And so, while some people believe that the approaching Shift to Oneness will be caused by an external earthly, or cosmic event; and others, an internal evolution; there are still others who believe that The Shift that people are speaking of will be caused by both. These people find truth in the familiar phrase "conflict breeds consciousness", and believe that many humans needs some major shifts in their outer physical reality in order to encourage them to make the Inner shift that will enable them to return to One.

Thus, it is thought by some adherents to this perspective that the physical events that are set to unfold in the next few months leading up to December 21, 2012, have been designed to escalate to such a dramatic level, that most of humanity will be faced with the possibility of their own death, and the loss of everything that they have worked to achieve in the material world, all of which would occur for the Divine Purpose of shifting humanity's perspective from the physical to the spiritual.

For in a world where so many are living only for material achievement and survival, it will not be until that material reality is threatened with extinction, and when money and luxury fail to satisfy our needs for peace and comfort, that the majority of people will awaken to the worthlessness of material wealth and success, and thereby be inspired to seek INWARDS to find a new purpose and meaning for life. And in doing so, many will finally understand the words that they have been uttering for so long which state that, "we are not human beings having a spiritual experience, but rather we are spiritual beings having a human experience."

And thus, when the events of the next few months have served their Divine Purpose, when the death and destruction have shaken us from our material obsessions, and given birth to our awareness of the Eternal Spirit that connects us all, we will learn to see the world in a new way; where even Death and Destruction, which humanity has denied and feared for so long, are seen to have a place and a purpose for which to be thankful and loving.

And as these increasingly intense events unfold in the coming months, they will teach humanity the lessons of pride and humility, by demonstrating the futility of our efforts to control the world outside of ourselves. And when people finally tire of wishing that the world was something that it isn't, and when they learn to be at peace with the way things are for they see it all as part of the Divine Plan, then may they also learn to see that exerting one's personal will to try to stop these events from happening would be like trying to stop others from having the same opportunity for learning.

For, it is our selfishness, and our ignorant use of free will that has brought us collectively into our present state of existence. Therefore, perhaps it is only by a 180 degree reversal, through selflessness, through the complete and utter surrender of ourselves and our *personal will* to the Divine Will of the Tao, that we may allow the forces of true change, and redemption, to work through us and liberate us completely from the unholy illusion of this world.

And for this reason, some believe that it will be the tremendous Shifting of *Outer events* in the months between now and December 21st, 2012, that will inspire humanity's INNER shift; helping them realize that we cannot, nor are we meant to change our outer world in order to find peace; but rather we are urged to turn inwards to seek and find the eternal peace that comes when one learns to see the Divine purpose and perfection of All.

And it is with this unified perspective of existence that one learns to relinquish 'my will' for 'Thy Will'; thereby realigning themselves with The Divine Will, and marking their long-awaited 'Return to One.'

The Darkness Before the Dawn

Having thus considered how Shifting one's perspective from the material to the spiritual, may serve to open one's eyes to the oneness of all, let us now consider what sort of events could unfold in the next few months that might assist humanity in its evolution from a purely material-based perspective of existence to one more rooted in spirituality.

As mentioned before, there are many people in the world today who because of their focus on material success and survival, will not spare a second thought for their soul or spiritual self, until they are faced with death, suffering and the inevitable collapse of everything they have come to depend on in the material world. Thus, in accordance with the familiar phrase that "it is always darkest before the dawn" it is possible that in the coming months the world may be required to experience a level of death and destruction that will encourage its material-obsessed inhabitants to return to a more spiritual-based perspective of existence.

And though it's understandable that the collapse of our material world and its systems could be quite a frightening experience; it is essential to understand here that those who learn to have Faith in the spiritual purpose of these events, will be given the tools and awareness that will allow them to face and flow through all of the challenges of the coming shift in relative grace and ease.

We have been told that "Faith is the Key." For when one learns to see that all beings and events exist for the Divine Purpose of encouraging us to seek and find that eternal PEACE INSIDE with 'the way things are', then we may learn to see that all is, in fact, serving the divine, and therefore All IS divine. And with this perspective, one may learn to move through the events of the coming months with a heart full of love and gratitude, rather than being consumed by hate and fear.

And it is the power of this Faith to bring us peace that is being referred to in the Hopi Prophecy of the Blue and Red Kachinas when it says "Life will get very perverted, and there will be little social order in these times. Many will ask for the mountains themselves to fall upon them, just to end their misery. While still others will appear as if untouched by what is occurring. For they are the ones who remember the original teachings and who have reconnected their hearts and spirit."

Having thus remembered the divine role that darkness may play in our spiritual evolution; let us now explore some of the potential challenges that could unfold in the next few months that might assist our souls' Journey 'back to one.'

And remember here, that it is not the intention with this essay to prophecy events as they are "going to occur", for the nature of prophecy ensures that our future is always changing, in accordance with our willingness to learn new lessons and perspectives. That said, our intention herein is to merely present some possibilities of what events *could* occur that might lead to the collapse of the material world as we know it, and to humanity's subsequent return to a spirit-based consciousness... and the resulting remembrance of the Oneness of all.

Though to many people, whose perspective of the state of our world is molded by popular news and media, the idea that our entire material reality could collapse in the months between now and December 21st, 2012 might seem like a sensationalist Hollywood film; what so few people realize, is that the process is already well underway.

In truth, a simple series of events whose elements are already in place, could cause the toppling of our existing world systems within as little as a week, or ten days. And though it may not look exactly like this, this is how an almost unimaginable series of seemingly dark and destructive events could serve to help all the souls of the Earth complete the long Journey Home, back to one.

All it would take is another staged terrorist attack in an American city, similar to that of 9/11; except this time rather than airplanes, the damage would be delivered by a device called a

Suitcase Nuke, which is a hypothetical suitcase-sized nuclear bomb, which has begun to receive a lot of mention in films and news reports within the popular media.

If such a bomb were to go off in an American city, and the authorities were to link its creation to Iran, whom the US is wrongfully accusing of developing Nuclear Weapons, in the same way that it accused Iraq of developing Weapons of Mass Destruction, this would pave the way for a US-Led Allied attack on Iran; which would then mark the official beginning of World War III.

In truth this war has already begun with US-Led Trade Sanctions against Iran being imposed by the United Nations, in an effort to cripple the country's military and economic production while the US and its allies make preparations for war. It is also known that for some months now the US has been amassing troops and weapons in Israel, in preparations for a massive offensive in the Middle East.

However, with the US having recently reached its 14.3 trillion dollar debt ceiling; with the dollar flagging, and the Euro near collapse, and with the US already over-extending itself in wars in Iraq, Afghanistan, Libya and Pakistan it's decision to engage in a world war, along with the crippling effects of the staged terrorist attack, would crush whatever faith remained in the US Markets and result in the collapse of the American Dollar; which would in turn begin the spiraling collapse of all of the world economies.

With world Oil Prices hovering at record highs, the Iranian President has promised that as soon as the first bomb drops on Iran he will set the oil fields on fire. Thus, with the value of the Euro and the Dollar dropped through the floor, the flaming oil fields would result in the sky-rocketing of Gas Prices; which would then lead to the inability to transport food and other goods around the world.

Statistics indicates that without steady transport, most urban centers would be depleted of food and resources within 3 days... and as quickly as that, the world would be changed forever.

However, there is much research, which indicates that these are just the beginning of a series of progressively intense, and unfathomable events that have been designed to be so shocking that many people who are completely unaware of them will be desperate for any form of salvation. And it will be at the point of humanity's greatest desperation, that those who have orchestrated these events will provide one self-serving solution. And that is to Unite the globe under the authority of a New World Order.

Here, our existing political, economic and military institutions would unite under a One World Government, One World Economy and One World Religion; which would offer to meet the immediate needs of humanity, providing food, money and medicine, and even 'miracles'; in exchange for complete obedience and subservience to the system.

However it is essential to understand here, that even though the voice calling people to the New World Order may use the appealing words of Unity, Truth and Service; it will only be offering a temporary solution to the _symptoms_ of humanity's suffering, along with promises to preserve a degree of comfort and security within a familiar system; where people are divided by the old-world perspectives of good and evil, rich and poor, strong and weak. This voice will speak to people's fears, and to their desires to protect and preserve the self.

And all those who choose, out of fear, to cling to the material, and continue their support of a ruling elite who have proven their lack of caring for the world and its inhabitants; will by the quality of their own thoughts and emotions, be required to experience increasingly more hardships until such a time that they are willing to put their Faith in the Divine Spirit, rather than the corrupt institutions of Man, or his false gods.

So what sort of events could unfold in the next few months that might bring the world to such a state of desperation that it would agree to Uniting the planet under the authority of a New World Order?

Should events similar to those mentioned previously occur, it is possible that the desperation caused by global food shortages and the collapse of the world's economies, could lead to worldwide pandemonium as cities erupt in mass riots and looting, while people rise against each other and their governments, in a desperate attempt to acquire food and resources for themselves and their families. This violence would be greatly compounded by the threat of nuclear war and invading forces that would be escalating around the world.

Add to this, the hysteria that would be caused if the Earth was shrouded in the three days of darkness prophesied by numerous cultures around the world, that most people didn't know would end. And then add another devastating earthquake, which would cause the meltdown of 30 nuclear reactors around the planet; whose radioactive wastes would spill into the earth's air and oceans.

And then, at the point when the entire world seemed divided and at war with each other, and when the state of humanity seemed all but lost, we would hear news reports of a strange object approaching from space, which was previously thought to be a Comet; but which upon its approach news reports would deceivingly tell us, is actually an alien spaceship.

Chapter 23

And to the world's surprise, from this ship would come fake alien invaders to attack the earth. Whose superior weapons and technology, actually created by our own world's military, would cause much damage and loss of life. And the world's leaders professing themselves to be greatly overmatched would have only one choice to save the planet... and that would be to unite the world's military forces.

With the entire planet reeling from war and the effects of the devastating earthquakes caused by the Prophesied return of a mysterious "Red Star", people all over the world would be praying for a miracle; when all of sudden their prayers would be answered. Somehow the earth's allied forces would miraculously defeat the aliens in a staged final battle; seemingly through their own military might, or with assistance from other aliens, either "real or fake", or even through the supernatural assistance of a False Messiah-like figure.

And when the world' allied forces, destroy the approaching ship which was once thought to be a blue comet, we would see the fulfillment of the ninth and last sign of the Hopi Prophecies, indicating that we have arrived at the end times, which reads: "You will hear of a dwelling-place in the heavens, above the earth, that shall fall with a great crash. It will appear as a blue star. Very soon after this, the ceremonies of my people will cease. For very soon afterward, The Red Star Kachina will return, and he shall bring with him the dawn of the fifth world."

With the Alien threat defeated, a broken and battered humanity would still have to deal with the wrath and destruction caused by the approaching Red Star Kachina. And thus, in the wake of humanity's staged victory, and in the face of oncoming threats, the world's United Nations would, in show of false goodwill, speak of the Oneness of Humanity and call for the unification of the world under a One World Government.

All of the world's debts would be erased, and a new global currency would be created, of which everyone would be offered a set number of credits, in exchange for their willingness to keep working for the selfsame system of governance and authority. Anyone wishing to receive these cash credits, food supplies and medical care from this One World System would be required to get a microchip implant that would allow their movements and I.D. to be tracked, and all those who do not comply with the rules and regulations of the system would simply have their chip deactivated.

And at the top of this New World Order, at the capstone of its pyramid of control, would be the "false savior"; which could appear either as an alien being, or as a luminous messiah-like figure who would perform signs and miracles so great that they may deceive, if that were possible, even the elect. And though this figure may have played a role in assisting humanity through its hardships, either with the fake alien invasion, or by performing miracles of medicine or technology its deception will be obvious.

For rather than inspiring humanity to see the Divine In All, this god with all its wonders and miracles would have humanity focus its worship on one supposedly divine being, or institution; thereby reserving a space for the old world divisions of 'right' and 'wrong', 'good' and 'evil'; and the worship of this thing would be most likely controlled by our present day ruling elite and popular spiritual leaders who would place themselves in between humanity and this fake god.

As fantastical as all this may sound there is much compelling evidence that points to the possibility of such events occurring, even those as extraordinary as the "fake alien invasion"; the possibility of which is being planted in peoples' minds through the noticeably high number of alien invasion movies and television shows that have come out in the last year, including the Recent National Geographic Series called "When the Aliens Attack"; which shows how the world's military forces would face and defeat a hostile alien invasion, not if... but when it happens.

And here it is essential to realize that compliance with the New World Order is a trap, just as surely as wishing harm upon those responsible for its creation. For both are reactions of fear. However if one is able to remember that all of this death and destruction is actually serving the divine purpose of shifting us from a material-based consciousness, to one founded more on spiritual awareness, then we may break away from the fearful reactions of compliance and resistance and take our first steps down the path towards the "original way" mentioned in the Hopi Prophecies, where everything is seen as One and sacred.

For if we can learn to see that those whom we would perceive as dark, or evil, are in fact serving us, by providing experiences that are essential on our path to self-realization; then perhaps it is also possible to see that in fact they are us, or at least an essential part of us, just as we are a part of them.

This vision of Oneness is reflected in the words of Rumi when he says: "Out beyond ideas of wrongdoing and right-doing, there is a field. I'll meet you there. When the soul lies down in that grass, the world is too full to talk about. Ideas, language, even the phrase 'each other' doesn't make sense anymore."

With this perspective, one may realize that all of the world's heightened chaos and conflict isn't actually the creation of one diabolical individual or organization, but rather in accordance with the Universal Wisdom "As above, So Below", it is an exact reflection, or projection, of the mounting conflict raging in the hearts and souls of the collective mind; where so many individual souls, who are wishing to move beyond this meaningless material existence, still feel powerless do so.

However, when we see the destruction of these systems which will no longer be able to support our needs, and when our leaders whom we have relied on to keep us safe, start a war that we realize could destroy the entire planet, those who have felt trapped by the system will finally 'let go' of their dependency on it, and seek a new way of living that is more in line with their inner heart's urge for peace and harmony. And thus, through the actions of those whom we would perceive to be 'dark', or 'evil', we will have learned, and been freed.

And in accordance with the perfection of this divine plan, our ability to love and recognize our oneness, with those whom some would call our oppressors, will be the power that sets those 'oppressors' free as well. For the prophesied return of the Red Star will open up the Book of Life, where the thoughts and deeds of every living being throughout creation are recorded for all to see.

And here every soul will have the opportunity to experience the suffering that it has caused through the course of its lives. And as those whom many would call their oppressors scan through their experiences, they will see how the hurt that they have caused is met with hate, anger and with thoughts of revolution and murder, and they will feel justified in their cruelty. However, as they continue their search deeper into the Book of Life, they will come across those, who even though they suffered greatly at their hands, have felt only love.

And it will be at this moment, that those souls which previously knew only hate, will learn the spiritual truth that a person can be redeemed just as surely by getting love, as they can by giving love. And by thus learning to love and be loved, we will rise above the challenges of this dark night of the soul, to meet the dawn of the glorious resurrection; and thereby we will have completed the long Journey Home, together... as one.

* * *

Keith Wyatt is the co-founder of the conscious media collective Awakening As One; a group of artists, who since May of 2010, have committed the total sum of their love, willingness and creativity into the production and presentation of high quality films intended to assist the ONE HEART and MIND of creation in navigating these days of great change, known to many as "The Shift of Ages." Awakening As One's films may be viewed by visiting: www.AwakeningAsOne.com Keith Wyatt may be found by contacting In The Garden Publishing.

CPSIA information can be obtained at www.ICGtesting.com
Printed in the USA
BVOW040031040912

299357BV00007B/46/P